TRADE ISSUES, POLICIES AND LAWS

TRADE CAPACITY BUILDING

ANALYSES OF U.S. ASSISTANCE TO DEVELOPING COUNTRIES

TRADE ISSUES, POLICIES AND LAWS

Additional books in this series can be found on Nova's website under the Series tab.

Additional e-books in this series can be found on Nova's website under the e-book tab.

ibrary of Congress Cataloging-in-Publication Data

3N:978-1-63463-733-6

Published by Nova Science Publishers, Inc. † New York

TRADE ISSUES, POLICIES AND LAWS

TRADE CAPACITY BUILDING

ANALYSES OF U.S. ASSISTANCE TO DEVELOPING COUNTRIES

RICHARD T. ROYCE
EDITOR

nova publishers
New York

CONTENTS

PREFACE

Trade capacity building (TCB) is a form of development assistance provided by the United States and other countries to help developing countries participate in and benefit from global trade. Congress and the executive branch have identified TCB assistance as an important tool for U.S. trade and development policy based on evidence of the effectiveness of trade in reducing poverty and generating economic development and growth. From 2005 to 2010, 24 U.S. agencies provided more than $9 billion in trade capacity building assistance to help more than 100 countries reduce poverty, increase economic growth, and achieve stability through trade. This book discusses the extent to which U.S. Agency for International Development's (USAID) 2003 strategy guides USAID's TCB activities; and describes methods USAID uses to coordinate TCB efforts with other U.S. government agencies at home and abroad.

Chapter 1 - From 2005 to 2010, 24 U.S. agencies provided more than $9 billion in trade capacity building (TCB) assistance to help more than 100 countries reduce poverty, increase economic growth, and achieve stability through trade. To report on TCB funding, the U.S. government conducts an annual survey of agencies and publicly reports the data in a TCB database administered by the U.S. Agency for International Development (USAID). GAO examined (1) how agencies' TCB activities are aligned with the agencies' goals, (2) the extent to which the TCB database provides sufficient information on key trends and funding, and (3) the extent to which USAID monitors and evaluates the effectiveness of its TCB activities. GAO focused on the agencies that reported the most funding for TCB activities since 2005—the Departments of the Army and State, the Millennium Challenge Corporation (MCC), and USAID—and the Office of the U.S. Trade

Representative (USTR). GAO analyzed U.S. government data; reviewed agencies' strategic, budget, and program documents; and met with U.S. and foreign government officials in select countries.

Chapter 2 - Since at least 2001, the United States has provided TCB assistance to developing countries to help them participate in and benefit from global trade. Multiple agencies provide this assistance, which may include support for World Trade Organization accession, customs procedures improvement, or development of infrastructure such as ports and roads. In this report, GAO focuses primarily on USAID because it provided the most funding for TCB in fiscal year 2012 and has a formal strategy focused entirely on TCB. GAO was asked to review the strategy, which is more than a decade old. GAO was also asked to examine USAID efforts to coordinate TCB activities to ensure that the United States is fulfilling its commitment in the most effective way.

In this report, GAO (1) determines the extent to which USAID's 2003 strategy guides USAID's TCB activities and (2) describes methods USAID uses to coordinate TCB efforts with other U.S. government agencies at home and abroad. GAO analyzed agency documents, interviewed relevant officials, and conducted fieldwork in six countries in Africa and Asia, selected for their diverse stages of development and geographic locations.

Chapter 3 - Integration into the global economy can be a powerful force for economic growth and poverty reduction. In its recent *National Security Strategy,* the Bush administration established the goal of igniting a new era of global economic growth through free markets and free trade.

Trade and investment are the principal mechanisms through which global market forces—competition, human resource development, technology transfer, and technological innovation—generate growth in developing and developed countries. During the 1990s, developing countries that successfully integrated into the global economy enjoyed per capita income increases averaging 5 percent annually. However, countries that limited their participation in the global economy saw their economies decline.

Developing countries' overall share of global trade is increasing, and the flow of foreign direct investment to poor countries has grown rapidly. But this growth is concentrated in a few countries, and many of the poorest developing countries remain on the sidelines. Not surprisingly, development issues have become increasingly prominent in international trade negotiations. The Doha Development Agenda recognizes that continued multilateral trade liberalization is necessary to accelerate growth and reduce poverty in developing countries and that World Trade Organization (WTO) member countries must help developing countries build their capacity to take advantage of trade liberalization. USAID trade capacity building (TCB) assistance programs—$423 million in FY2001 and $476 million in FY2002—are already helping developing countries to integrate themselves into the global economy.

In: Trade Capacity Building
Editor: Richard T. Royce
ISBN: 978-1-63463-733-6

Chapter 1

FOREIGN ASSISTANCE: THE UNITED STATES PROVIDES WIDE-RANGING TRADE CAPACITY BUILDING ASSISTANCE, BUT BETTER REPORTING AND EVALUATION ARE NEEDED*

United States Government Accountability Office

WHY GAO DID THIS STUDY

From 2005 to 2010, 24 U.S. agencies provided more than $9 billion in trade capacity building (TCB) assistance to help more than 100 countries reduce poverty, increase economic growth, and achieve stability through trade. To report on TCB funding, the U.S. government conducts an annual survey of agencies and publicly reports the data in a TCB database administered by the U.S. Agency for International Development (USAID). GAO examined (1) how agencies' TCB activities are aligned with the agencies' goals, (2) the extent to which the TCB database provides sufficient information on key trends and funding, and (3) the extent to which USAID monitors and evaluates

* This is an edited, reformatted and augmented version of a United States Government Accountability Office publication, No. GAO-11-727, dated July 2011.

the effectiveness of its TCB activities. GAO focused on the agencies that reported the most funding for TCB activities since 2005—the Departments of the Army and State, the Millennium Challenge Corporation (MCC), and USAID—and the Office of the U.S. Trade Representative (USTR). GAO analyzed U.S. government data; reviewed agencies' strategic, budget, and program documents; and met with U.S. and foreign government officials in select countries.

WHAT GAO RECOMMENDS

GAO recommends that the Administrator of USAID publicly report identified limitations and key distinctions in the categories of TCB assistance in the database. GAO also recommends that USAID develop a written plan for using its recent TCB evaluation and for conducting evaluations on an ongoing basis. USAID stated that it has already taken steps consistent with the GAO recommendations.

WHAT GAO FOUND

USAID and State conduct TCB activities that are aligned with their primary goals, but TCB is secondary to the goals of other agencies. USAID and State have developed strategic plans that include TCB-focused goals. Aligned with these goals, USAID and State assist countries in negotiating and implementing trade agreements. In addition, USAID assists countries in taking advantage of economic growth opportunities stemming from trade, often in conjunction with other agency goals. TCB is not a primary focus of MCC and the Army, however, they conduct activities to meet their broader agency goals that have trade-related effects. MCC identifies trade-related assistance it considers TCB as part of its programs' poverty reduction goals. The Army implements TCB-related physical infrastructure projects as part of its disaster response objectives and in support of its reconstruction and economic development efforts in Iraq and Afghanistan.

The U.S. government TCB database has reported that annual TCB funding has increased from $1.35 billion in 2005 to $1.69 billion in 2010, but the database does not adequately describe certain factors underlying this growth and other significant changes in the composition of TCB funding. From 2005 to 2010, two agencies—MCC and the Army—began reporting significant TCB funding, primarily for physical infrastructure projects. Their funding comprised 54 percent of total TCB, and physical infrastructure projects comprised 45 percent of total TCB. However, the TCB database does not adequately explain significant factors driving changes in the composition of TCB funding. In particular, the annual TCB survey methodology attempts to identify and quantify just the trade-related components of projects, but this can be difficult in practice, particularly for physical infrastructure projects. Although GAO found the survey data to be generally reliable, these factors can lead to limitations in the data that are not described for its users. Clear reporting and transparent methodology and data collection are essential to understanding levels of funding and changes in the nature of TCB over time.

USAID has improved its assessment of TCB activities, including developing performance indicators and taking the positive step of commissioning a multicountry evaluation of the effects of TCB, but it has yet to develop plans to make use of the evaluation's valuable insights. USAID uses trade and investment indicators to assess the immediate results of its TCB activities. However, officials explained that it is difficult to attribute trade-related trends revealed by the indicators to the effects of TCB assistance and collect valid and reliable data to measure progress. To assess longer-term results, USAID has commissioned evaluations of TCB programs in specific countries, but these are limited in number. It recently commissioned a multicountry evaluation of the long-term effectiveness of its TCB activities agencywide. While USAID is beginning to incorporate the evaluation's results in its training, it has yet to develop plans for disseminating best practices to missions and offices on the methods they may use to better manage and assess their activities. Furthermore, it has not made plans for conducting evaluations on an ongoing basis.

ABBREVIATIONS

AGOA	African Growth and Opportunity Act of 2000
Army	Department of the Army
CAFTA-DR	Central America-Dominican Republic Free Trade Agreement
CERP	Commander's Emergency Response Program
FTA	free trade agreement
LDC	least-developed country
MCC	Millennium Challenge Corporation

OECD	Organization for Economic Cooperation and Development
State	Department of State
TIFA	Trade and Investment Framework Agreement
TCB	trade capacity building
TPSC	Trade Policy Staff Committee
USAID	U.S. Agency for International Development
USTR	Office of the U.S. Trade Representative
WTO	World Trade Organization

* * *

July 29, 2011

The Honorable Howard L. Berman
Ranking Member
Committee on Foreign Affairs
House of Representatives

The Honorable Joseph Crowley
House of Representatives

The Honorable Jim McDermott
House of Representatives

Trade capacity building (TCB) is a form of development assistance provided by the United States and other countries to help developing countries participate in and benefit from global trade. Congress and the executive branch have identified TCB assistance as an important tool for U.S. trade and development policy based on evidence of the effectiveness of trade in reducing poverty and generating economic development and growth. According to the Office of the U.S. Trade Representative (USTR), poverty rates for countries engaged in international trade have fallen sharply over the last 20 years. In the context of the ongoing Doha Development Agenda multilateral trade negotiations of the World Trade Organization (WTO), WTO member countries have recognized the impact of trade on development, including the role that trade can play in reducing poverty, achieving economic growth, and raising income levels. WTO members have also recognized the importance of trade-related assistance for addressing the constraints that limit the ability of developing countries and, in particular the least-developed countries, to fully benefit from trade and the rules-based multilateral trading system. To respond to these concerns, in 2001 and 2005, the WTO affirmed the importance of TCB assistance and the United States and other donors pledged continued support, respectively. The U.S. government provides TCB assistance to help developing countries worldwide build the physical, human, and institutional capacity to participate in global trade. Multiple U.S. agencies have developed a variety of programs that provide such assistance and support more than 100 countries. When we examined U.S. government TCB efforts in 2005, we noted the importance of the linkages between trade and development and recommended that more evaluation be performed to help ensure that TCB activities are effective in helping countries benefit from trade. We also cited the importance of evaluation in demonstrating that the capacity building goals envisioned by the United States are being achieved.[1]

In response to your interest in U.S. TCB programs, this report examines (1) how agencies' TCB activities are aligned with the agencies' goals, (2) the extent to which the U.S. government TCB database provides sufficient information on key trends and funding, and (3) the extent to which the U.S. Agency for International Development (USAID) monitors and evaluates the effectiveness of its TCB activities.

To address these objectives, we analyzed available data from the U.S. government TCB database, which is maintained by USAID and reports annual TCB data using a governmentwide survey. We have assessed these data as part of our previous and ongoing work and have determined that they are sufficiently reliable to identify TCB funding by agency, country, and category; although we found limitations to the use of the data, as discussed in this report. We focused our review on TCB activities provided by the Departments of the Army (Army) and State (State), the Millennium Challenge Corporation (MCC),[2] and USAID, which together have funded more than 90 percent of total U.S. TCB assistance from fiscal years 2005 to 2010. In addition, we included USTR in our focus due to its unique trade policy role. In conducting our work, we analyzed strategic, budget, and programmatic documents describing these agencies' TCB funding and activities. We reviewed data and information these agencies use to measure the performance of their activities and, where available, evaluations of programs or projects. We conducted fieldwork in Colombia, Morocco, and Mozambique. We selected these countries because they were among the 10 countries receiving the most TCB funding from fiscal years 2005 to 2009. In addition, we sought a mix of U.S. agencies providing assistance in-country and the categories of assistance provided, as well as geographic diversity. In each country we reviewed agencies' strategy documents, and performance plans and reports. We also interviewed agency officials, host government officials, and contracted implementing partners and visited TCB projects.

We conducted this performance audit from July 2010 through July 2011 in accordance with generally accepted auditing standards. Those standards require that we plan and perform the audit to obtain sufficient, appropriate evidence to provide a reasonable basis for our findings and conclusions based on our audit objectives. We believe that the evidence obtained provides a reasonable basis for our findings and conclusions based on our audit objectives. Appendix I contains a more detailed description of our scope and methodology.

BACKGROUND

TCB assistance is based on the premise that international trade can positively benefit a country's overall growth and development. The United States and other countries increasingly view TCB assistance as an important tool in promoting economic growth and reducing poverty. Expanding trade with and among developing countries can be a critical driver of economic growth and poverty reduction because it encourages entrepreneurship, human resource development, technology transfer, technological innovation, and good governance.

Developing countries have increasingly integrated into the global trading system, and some of those countries have become important U.S. trading partners. According to the World Bank, exports from developing countries have grown twice as fast as those of high-income countries since 2000. Moreover, imports in developing countries grew at almost twice the rate of high-income countries. As a result, developing countries account for a growing share of world imports. Furthermore, since 2000, many developing countries have acceded to the WTO.[3] Currently, about two-thirds of WTO members are developing countries or least-developed countries.[4] In addition, many developing countries have entered into free trade agreements (FTA) with the United States. FTAs phase out barriers to trade in goods with particular countries or groups of countries and contain rules designed to improve access in services, investment, and intellectual property rights.

However, many developing countries—in particular the least developed—face constraints that severely limit their ability to implement trade agreements and benefit from trade. Many developing countries lack the physical, institutional, or human capacity to participate effectively in global trade. Additionally, developing countries sometimes lack the financial and human resources to fulfill their trade commitments. USTR has indicated that TCB assistance is important to enable developing countries to negotiate and implement market-opening and reform-oriented trade agreements. In addition, some view TCB assistance as important to securing broad-based reforms across countries so that all countries benefit from the trade rules negotiated in the WTO and in other trade agreements. In 2001, the WTO Doha Ministerial Declaration advised that technical assistance should be designed to assist developing, least-developed, and low-income countries to meet their WTO obligations, and draw on the benefits of an open, rules-based multilateral trading system. The WTO created the Doha Development Agenda Global Trust Fund to help developing countries build capacity and establish a reliable basis for funding WTO-related technical assistance. The 2005 Hong Kong WTO Ministerial Declaration called for the expansion and improvement of this type of assistance and set in motion a process to achieve this known as the Aid-for-Trade Initiative.[5] Partnering with the WTO on this initiative, the Organization for Economic Cooperation and Development (OECD) jointly created a database to provide comprehensive information on bilateral donor and multilateral/regional agency support for TCB. The OECD has issued a number of reports on aid-for-trade issues and attempts to share good practices so that developing countries can capitalize on the opportunities of international trade.

To identify and quantify the U.S. government's TCB activities in developing and transitional economies, USAID conducts an annual survey on behalf of USTR. The data gathered from this survey are used to inform and respond to inquiries from Congress, the executive branch, the general public, and multilateral organizations such as the WTO. USTR officials use the database regularly and, according to these officials, it is a useful tool for identifying U.S. agencies' TCB activities and funding in a particular country or region, as well as the full extent of assistance the U.S. government provides in that area. USAID oversees a contractor that collects and maintains the survey results in a publicly available online database. The survey defines TCB and asks agencies to place their assistance into a range of categories and estimate funding obligated for each category (table 1 provides further information on these categories). In addition to administering this survey, USAID is also tasked with reviewing completed survey forms, and checking for accuracy and consistency in the reporting of funding and allocation into TCB categories. A variety of U.S. agencies have a role in providing TCB assistance, including the Departments of State, the Army, Labor, the Treasury, and Commerce; MCC; and USAID.

Table 1. U.S. TCB Categories and Definitions

Category	Definition
WTO awareness, participation, and accession	Assistance to help governments and private sector institutions benefit from membership in the WTO or to understand fully the benefits of membership, and assistance to help countries in the WTO accession process meet the requirements of accession.
WTO agreements	Assistance that enables countries to better participate in, and benefit from, particular WTO agreements.
Trade facilitation	Generally defined as assistance in lowering the costs of engaging in, and benefiting from, particular WTO agreements.
• Business services and training	Support to improve the associations and networks in the business sector, as well as to enhance the skills of business people engaged in trade.
• Export promotion	Assistance to increase market opportunities for developing country and transition economy producers.
• Customs operation and administration	Assistance to help countries modernize and improve their customs offices.
• E-commerce development and information technologies	Assistance to help countries acquire and use information technology to promote trade by creating business networks and disseminating market information.
• Regional trade agreements	Assistance to increase the ability of regional trade agreements and individual countries to facilitate trade and help potential regional trade agreement members.
• Other trade facilitation	Support that facilitates the flow of trade in other ways.
Human resource and labor standards	Assistance to support the enforcement of labor standards and workers rights, development of trade unions and dispute resolution mechanisms, strategies for workforce development and training, and the elimination of child labor.
Physical infrastructure development	Assistance to establish trade-related telecommunications, transport, ports, airports, power, water, and industrial zones.
Trade-related agricultural development	Support for trade-related aspects of the agriculture and agribusiness sectors.

Category	Definition
Environment sector trade and standards	Assistance to establish environmental standards or to promote environmental technology.
Governance, transparency and interagency coordination	Support for legal and institutional reform to improve governance and make policies more transparent as well as help government agencies function more effectively in the trade policy area.
Financial sector development and good governance	Support for financial sector work, monetary and fiscal policy, exchange rates, commodity markets, and capital markets.
Competition policy and foreign investment	Support for the design and implementation of antitrust laws, as well as of laws and regulations related to investment and investor protections.
Services trade development	Support to help developing countries increase their flows of trade in services.
• Tourism sector development	Assistance to help countries expand their international tourism sectors.
• Other services development	Assistance to help countries develop trade in services in all sectors other than tourism, including financial services, energy, transportation, and education.

Sources: USAID and USTR.

In our 2005 report on U.S. TCB efforts, focusing on the period from 2001 to 2004, we found that U.S. TCB assistance was primarily a collection of a variety of trade and development activities. We noted that 18 agencies had self-reported that they obligated almost $2.9 billion for TCB activities in more than 100 countries and that USAID provided 71 percent of overall U.S. TCB assistance.

We also found that the six agencies we reviewed were neither systematically monitoring nor measuring program performance in terms of TCB and recommended USAID and USTR develop a strategy to systematically monitor and measure results and evaluate effectiveness. In response, USAID, in consultation with USTR, took steps to develop a multicountry evaluation to measure the effectiveness of U.S. TCB assistance, which was issued in November 2010.

USAID AND STATE CONDUCT TCB ACTIVITIES ALIGNED WITH THEIR PRIMARY GOALS; TCB IS SECONDARY TO GOALS OF OTHER AGENCIES

Of the four agencies we reviewed that fund and implement TCB activities, only USAID and State have strategic plans that include TCB-focused goals. USAID has developed a strategic plan for TCB, and State's joint strategic plan with USAID for fiscal years 2007 to 2012 supports USAID's goal of advancing developing countries' participation in and benefits from trade agreements. MCC and the Army conduct TCB-related activities that support their broader strategic and agency mission goals. However, they do not have strategic plans and goals that specifically relate to TCB.

USAID and State Provide Assistance that Directly and Indirectly Supports USAID's TCB Strategic Plan

USAID and State have strategic goals specific to promoting TCB and have incorporated these goals in the planning of their assistance. (For further information on USAID's planning of its TCB activities, see app. II.) In 2003, USAID issued a formal strategic plan on TCB, to focus its TCB efforts and guide the selection of new activities.[6] The plan calls for USAID's TCB projects to support the three primary objectives of helping countries participate in trade negotiations, implement trade agreements, and take advantage of trade opportunities. In addition, State supports USAID's TCB efforts outlined in its strategy. The USAID and State joint strategic plan for fiscal years 2007 to 2012 calls for supporting USAID's strategic goal of providing assistance to help countries participate in and benefit from trade agreement negotiations. We found that USAID and State planned and provided assistance that supported TCB strategic objectives. USAID also provided assistance that aligns with its April 2008 strategy for economic growth that includes the goals of (1) developing well functioning markets in developing countries, primarily through supporting policy and regulatory reforms and (2) strengthening the international framework of policies and institutions that support countries' economic growth and opportunities by promoting international standards.

USAID and State Directly Support Participation in Trade Negotiations

USAID and State, in collaboration with other U.S. government agencies, have provided TCB assistance as part of USTR-created TCB working groups in developing countries where the United States is negotiating a FTA. (For further information on interagency efforts to coordinate TCB assistance, see app. III.) These working groups meet during the negotiations to identify and select TCB activities that assist developing country negotiating partners through regional and bilateral TCB programs. In particular, TCB working groups were a feature of the bilateral negotiations in support of the ratified Central America-Dominican Republic Free Trade Agreement (CAFTA-DR) and Peru FTA, and the signed FTAs with Colombia and Panama. For example:

- During the CAFTA-DR negotiations, USAID, State, and other U.S. agencies helped to provide technical assistance to the Central American countries to address a variety of trade capacity issues, including the strengthening of plant and animal health and food safety regulatory systems, and the strengthening of customs procedures.
- In conjunction with the U.S.-Colombian free trade negotiations a USAID program assisted the government of Colombia in adopting and implementing policy and regulatory reforms to facilitate the conclusion and implementation of the FTA. The program included 18 components of trade-related policy reforms that led to Colombia's development of new regulations and procedures consistent with the FTA's requirements.[7] For example, the program supported the establishment of a national food safety policy that ensured consistency with U.S. sanitary and phytosanitary[8] standards.

In addition, USAID provided TCB assistance to support countries' efforts to accede to the WTO. In fiscal year 2009, USAID provided TCB assistance supporting the accession and membership of nine countries to the WTO.[9] USAID's activities supported foreign governments' implementation of regulatory reforms and the adoption of domestic policies, laws, and regulations that align with international standards. For example, under a 5-year joint-funded program with State, USAID provided the government of Laos with legal and economic analysis of needed reforms, particularly in the areas of services, and intellectual property rights and standards.

USAID and State Directly Support the Implementation of Trade Agreements

USAID and State have provided TCB assistance to support the implementation of U.S. FTAs with developing country partners. The final texts of FTAs, including CAFTA-DR, and the Peru FTA, have provisions that created committees on TCB to assist partner countries in implementing the trade agreements and adjusting to more liberalized trade. USAID, State, and other U.S. agencies have provided TCB assistance in support of the work of these committees. For example, USAID's Regional Trade Program for CAFTA-DR provided training relevant to compliance with the provisions of the CAFTA-DR agreement, including training to some partner countries' foreign government officials, judicial officials, and private sector representatives in the area of intellectual property rights protections and investment regulations. The program also strengthened CAFTA-DR partner countries' customs operations and administration to meet international standards as well as the FTA's provisions.

USAID also conducts TCB activities with the objective of building the capacity of firms to capitalize on the benefits of FTAs. For instance, in 2005, USAID created a program to provide technical assistance to Moroccan firms in various sectors, including apparel, textiles, leather footwear, and processed foods, with the goal of developing business opportunities between the United States and Morocco under the U.S.- Morocco FTA. Under the program, Moroccan firms and trade associations received technical assistance, including seminars and workshops on a variety of trade-related topics such as sales planning, transport logistics, and production standards and certification.

USAID also assists countries in adopting requirements related to WTO agreements, and supports countries seeking to benefit from regional trade agreements. USAID funds and implements projects to help recipient countries comply with WTO agreements in areas such as government procurement, agriculture, the application of sanitary and phytosanitary measures, and the agreement on intellectual property rights.[10] In addition, USAID provided technical assistance to address developing countries' capacities for meeting standards under regional trade agreements. For example, a primary objective of USAID's Southern Africa Trade Hub is to increase international competitiveness and intraregional trade in the Southern African Development Community region.[11]

USAID Directly Supports Trade-Related Opportunities Provided under U.S. Trade Preference Programs

In addition, USAID provides TCB assistance in support of opportunities provided under trade preference programs, most prominently the African Growth and Opportunity Act of 2000 (AGOA).[12] To help countries take full advantage of increased trading opportunities under AGOA, USAID provides TCB assistance primarily through trade hubs in East, West, and Southern Africa and bilateral missions in sub-Saharan Africa. The trade hubs assisted firms in taking advantage of opportunities under AGOA by helping them develop market linkages, adapt products to the U.S. market, and facilitate business deals. One trade hub also developed national export strategies identifying countries' constraints and opportunities for exporting under AGOA, and another trade hub conducted workshops to help African firms and foreign government officials increase their understanding of AGOA.

USAID Indirectly Supports TCB in a Number of Ways

In conjunction with objectives other than TCB, USAID conducts TCB-related activities that indirectly support TCB by helping countries take advantage of trade-related economic opportunities. These activities aim to address a wide range of development needs in the public and private sectors. In conducting our fieldwork and research, we identified USAID projects that missions conducted for various objectives in addition to TCB, but that mission officials identified as achieving outcomes related to international trade:

- The mission in Mozambique conducted a TCB-related agriculture development program with the primary objective of increasing the sustainability and profitability of the country's private sector to strengthen rural income growth. While TCB was not an explicit objective, as part of the program, USAID funded a commercial food laboratory that provides screening services to reduce illnesses from contaminated local food supplies, which also helped producers meet quality standards for the export of commercial food products.
- USAID implemented TCB-related programs in Colombia with the primary objective of generating economic alternatives to illicit crop production. However, the program also helped agricultural producers expand sales, including exports, and assisted the government of Colombia in implementing economic policies and institutional reforms to enhance the competitiveness of the Colombian economy in general, including those related to international trade.

- In Morocco, the mission conducted TCB-related activities aimed at improving the general business environment and promoting broad-based economic growth, in part through a reduction in trade and investment barriers. One TCB-related program provided technical assistance in support of regulatory and legal reforms to promote investment and enhance the general ease of doing business, for instance. In addition, USAID implemented a program to improve the productivity and competitiveness of certain agricultural products, including those for export.

TCB Is Secondary to the Goals of MCC and the Army

Other agencies we reviewed do not have TCB-focused strategic goals, but conduct activities that have trade-related effects and that are considered TCB to fulfill their broader mission goals. While 23 other U.S. agencies, in addition to USAID, reported funding for TCB-related activities from fiscal years 2005 to 2010, MCC, in particular, reported obligating almost half of total U.S. government TCB funding over this period. In addition, over the same period, the Army reported obligating the fourth largest amount of funding for TCB among U.S. agencies, following MCC, USAID, and State. However, MCC and the Army do not have strategic plans and goals that specifically relate to TCB, but sometimes conduct TCB-related activities to fulfill their strategic and agency mission goals. MCC generally identifies TCB-related activities as part of its poverty reduction goals in its 5-year country compacts and threshold programs, although TCB is not an explicit objective.[13] The Army conducts trade-related physical infrastructure projects, such as roads and telecommunications projects, that it reports as TCB to respond to its emergency and disaster response objectives in Afghanistan and in support of its reconstruction efforts in Iraq and Afghanistan.

MCC' s TCB-Related Activities Are Part of Its Larger Mission to Reduce Poverty and Support Economic Growth

Although from 2005 to 2010 MCC reported obligating the largest amount of TCB-related assistance funding of any U.S. government agency—approximately $4.7 billion, or 65 percent, of its total assistance—MCC does not fund TCB-related activities for the specific objective of TCB, according to officials. It funds TCB activities as part of its larger mission to reduce poverty and stimulate economic growth through its compact agreements, and to help countries address policy weaknesses through its threshold programs. MCC provides monetary assistance through multiyear compact agreements with developing countries that create and maintain sound policy environments. Its threshold programs fund a limited amount of assistance to certain developing countries to help them become eligible for compact funding. TCB is not an explicit objective of the agreements and programs, according to officials, and MCC funds are not earmarked for specific TCB projects. Compact countries define their own development priorities and project proposals, which may include projects considered as TCB. MCC first reported obligating funding for TCB assistance when it signed its initial compacts with recipient countries in fiscal year 2005. MCC has continued to report high levels of funding for TCB assistance as countries sign compacts, but the levels of funding and types of TCB-related activities depend on whether countries include TCB as a component in their proposals.

MCC operates differently than USAID and other U.S. agencies in that it only provides assistance to developing countries based on criteria involving governance and economic reform measures. For a country to be selected as eligible for MCC's compact assistance program, it must have demonstrated a commitment to ruling justly, encouraging economic freedom, and investing in people by performing well on 17 indicators that MCC uses to assess policy performance. Each compact is unique, and MCC works in partnership with eligible countries that identify the greatest constraints to their own development and establish priorities. In consultation with the private sector and nongovernmental organizations, a country government submits a proposal that may include TCB-related projects. The proposal forms the basis for the compact. To help focus the proposal on the root causes of constraints to private investments and identify the appropriate activities, MCC and country partners use a written analysis of a country's constraints. The analyses facilitate the consultative process for developing compacts that address country priorities. For example, according to MCC officials in Mozambique, MCC funded prefeasibility analyses of four potential TCB-related projects. Three of the projects were included in the compact. However, following consultations, a free trade zone project was determined not to be viable.

As of fiscal year 2010, MCC reported TCB-related activities in 20 compact countries and 9 threshold program countries.[14] TCB-related activities in compact countries primarily consisted of physical infrastructure development activities, while activities in threshold program countries focused on customs operation and administration, such as strengthening border inspections to improve import and export monitoring. For example, in Benin,

Honduras, Mali, Mozambique, and Tanzania, MCC has funded a variety of physical infrastructure projects, including port and airport improvement projects, as well as road construction and rehabilitation. The Moldova, Sao Tome and Principe, and Zambia threshold programs included a variety of activities related to customs operations and administration, including the upgrading and modernization of customs systems and enhancements to custom operations and inspection procedures.

The Army's TCB-Related Activities Support Infrastructure Development in Iraq and Afghanistan

The Army does not have TCB-focused strategic objectives, according to Army officials. However, the Army funds trade-related physical infrastructure projects considered TCB as part of the Commander's Emergency Response Program in Afghanistan and in support of its infrastructure development efforts in both Iraq and Afghanistan.[15] Since fiscal year 2009, the Army has reported $615 million in total obligated funding for TCB-related activities that support the Army's broader goal to achieve U.S. security objectives, provide basic humanitarian aid and services, and support economic stability and development as a means of responding to security concerns. For example, as part of its funding for humanitarian assistance, the Army constructed and restored a variety of physical infrastructure in Afghanistan that it reported contributed to trade, including telecommunications and electrical systems projects. Although the objectives of these projects are not directly focused on TCB, according to officials of one Army command, these projects further increase economic integration and trade by providing communication and electrical power linkages between Afghanistan and neighboring countries. The Army also undertook food production and distribution processes in Afghanistan that also helped meet sanitary and phytosanitary standards. In addition, as part of its mission, the Army supports economic stability and sustainable development to promote security, in part, through the development of infrastructure, such as roads, that facilitate trade. For example, the Army funded the restoration and construction of roads in 20 regions in Afghanistan, which it reported contributed to the development of physical infrastructure needed to promote trade. In addition, the Army reported funding to repair, improve, and create new infrastructure in Iraq and Afghanistan, including roads and bridges, necessary for trade routes and market access improvements. According to officials of one Army command, the road projects facilitated regional and international trade flows by linking Afghanistan with neighboring countries. Officials noted that recipient countries of the Army's assistance are identified through Department of Defense guidance and with input from in-country U.S. agencies on recipient countries' needs.

The TCB Database Does Not Provide Adequate Information Necessary to Understand Significant Changes in the Composition of Reported TCB Activities

USAID does not adequately describe certain key factors underlying significant changes in the composition of TCB funding as reported by the TCB database. According to the database, from 2005 to 2010, overall annual funding increased 25 percent, from $1.35 billion to $1.69 billion. This increase is largely the result of the inclusion of funding from MCC beginning in 2005, and the Army beginning in 2009. Correspondingly, there has been a steep decline in the share of total funding reported by USAID and other agencies. MCC and the Army reported TCB funding primarily in the category of physical infrastructure, which has contributed to a steep rise in overall funding in that category.[16]

In addition, agencies that are newly identified for inclusion in the database, such as the Army, are sometimes unable to provide data for previous years, which may imply a certain amount of under reporting. Although the annual TCB survey attempts to identify and quantify just the trade-related components of projects, this can be difficult for officials to fully achieve in practice. It may also be challenging for survey administrators to fully clarify the distinction between direct and indirect TCB funding. The limitations involved in collecting and reporting TCB-related data do not necessarily invalidate the figures in the database; however, USAID is not providing sufficient context or explanation of these limiting factors with the dataset.

Clear reporting and transparency in methodology and collection are essential for users of the data to understand changes in the nature of TCB over time.

The Inclusion of MCC and the Army Has Significantly Increased the Reported Levels of and Changed the Composition of Total TCB Funding

Since our previous review of TCB assistance in 2005, there have been significant changes in the level and composition of total TCB funding as reported by the U.S. TCB database. Our past report reviewed TCB funding obligated from 2001 to 2004. Over that period, the average annual amount reported by all agencies was about $735 million. In comparison the average annual amount reported by agencies during the period 2005–2010 was more than twice as much—$1.65 billion. From 2005 to 2010, total funding levels have generally increased, with annually reported funding growing from $1.35 billion to $1.69 billion, a 25 percent increase. Since 2005, the number of agencies reporting TCB obligations has grown from 18 to 24. However, the significant increase in total TCB funding is attributable to two agencies in particular—MCC, which was established in 2004 and began reporting TCB funding in 2005, and the Army, which began reporting TCB funding in 2009 (see fig. 1).

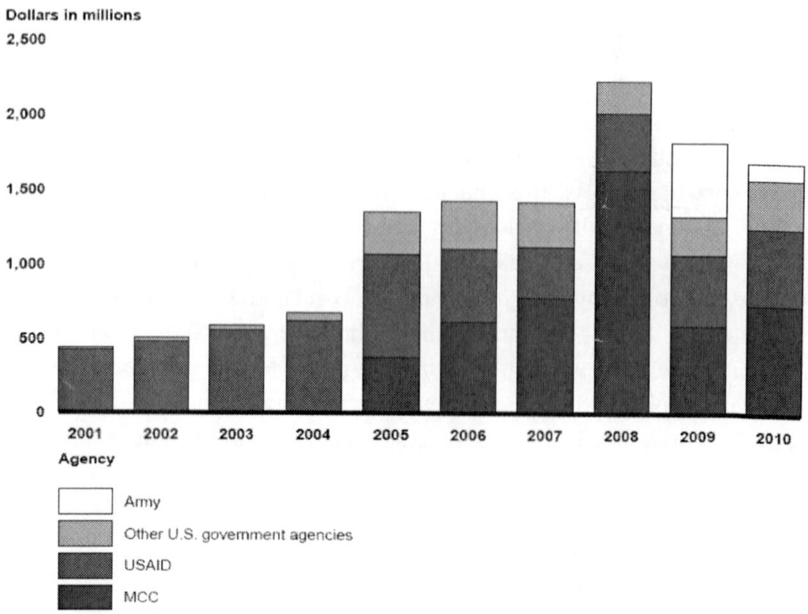

Source: GAO analysis of U.S. government TCB database.

Figure 1. U.S. TCB Funding by Agency, Fiscal Years 2001–2010.

Over 2005–2010, MCC reported obligating $4.7 billion, or 48 percent of total TCB funding. In 2009, the first year Army began submitting data to the survey, it reported $497 million in funding or 27 percent of the total for that year. Combined funding from MCC and Army comprised 54 percent of total TCB over 2005–2010. The significant amount of funding reported by MCC and the Army lowered the relative share of total TCB funding provided by USAID and other agencies. For example, over 2001–2004, USAID reported obligating 70 percent of total TCB funding, the largest share of any U.S. agency; while over 2005–2010, USAID's share declined to 29 percent of total funding. While the amount of TCB funding provided by USAID declined over that period, this does not account for such a large decline in relative share. In addition, the relative combined share of total funding for all other U.S. agencies also declined, going from 25 percent over 2001–2004 to 10 percent over 2005–2010.

Annual TCB funding in the category of physical infrastructure has grown from $346 million in 2005 to $787 million in 2010, a 127 percent increase. Over 2005–2010, physical infrastructure was the largest category of total TCB funding, at 45 percent of the total, or $4.5 billion out of $9.9 billion. In contrast, over 2001–2004, physical infrastructure comprised only 8 percent of total funding, or $226 million out of $2.9 billion. The share of funding for all other TCB categories has declined between those two periods. For example, there has been a decline in the overall share of funding of trade facilitation, which was the largest category over 2001– 2004, from 27 percent to 16 percent, and a decline from 17 to 6 percent in human resources and labor standards, which was previously the second largest category. Figure 2 illustrates the large increase in the category of physical infrastructure and the proportional decline in the other categories of TCB, from 2001–2004 to 2005–2010.

The increase in the category of physical infrastructure since 2005 has been driven by the TCB funding reported by MCC and the Army. Physical infrastructure and trade-related agriculture constitute the primary categories of TCB assistance obligated by MCC. Over 2005–2010, MCC reported obligating $3.3 billion in the category of physical infrastructure development and $667 million in trade-related agriculture. MCC's funding made up a majority share of overall TCB funding for both categories. MCC accounts for 74 percent of total funding in physical infrastructure and for more than half of total funding in trade-related agriculture. Similarly, the $497 million in TCB funding reported by the Army in 2009 was exclusively for physical infrastructure development. This amount accounts for 13 percent of total funding in physical infrastructure, the majority of which—$396 million—the Army reported as funding for road and bridge projects in Afghanistan. Figure 3 shows the amount of funding for each category of TCB by agency over 2005–2010.

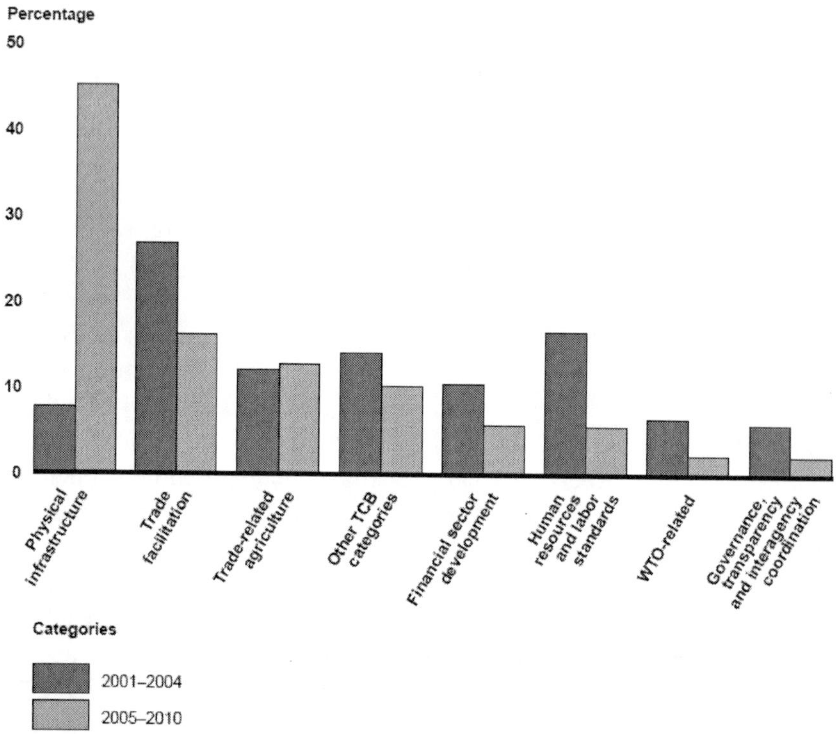

Source: GAO analysis of U.S. government TCB database.

Note: Other TCB categories included environmental sector trade and standards, competition policy and foreign investment incentives, and services trade development including tourism.

Figure 2. Shares of Total U.S. TCB Funding by Category, Fiscal Years 2001–2004 and 2005–2010.

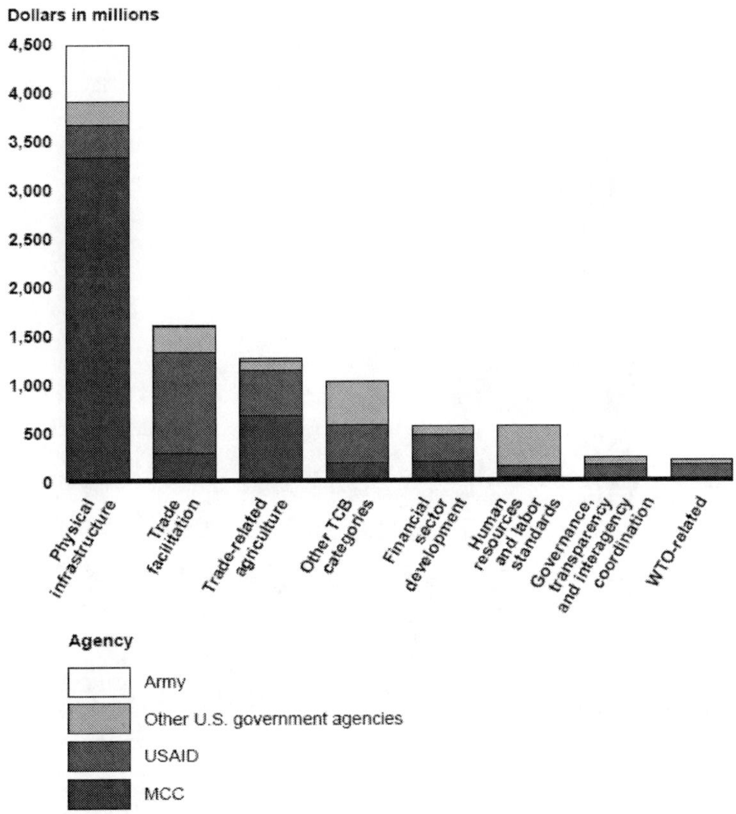

Source: GAO analysis of U.S. government TCB database.

Figure 3. TCB Funding by Category and Agency, Fiscal Years 2005–2010..

MCC and the Army have also impacted the regional distribution of TCB as reported by the database. Since 2005, U.S. agencies have provided TCB funding to 143 recipient countries in 6 geographic regions, including Southern Asia, Europe and Eurasia, East Asia/Oceania, Latin America and the Caribbean, the Middle East and North Africa, and sub-Saharan Africa. The sub-Saharan African region received the most funding, driven primarily by projects funded by MCC (see fig. 4). Funding for Southern Asia was largely made up of the Army's reported 2009 funding of physical infrastructure projects in Afghanistan. In contrast, USAID funding is spread more evenly worldwide. (For a more detailed table of country funding, including TCB assistance to least developed countries, see app. IV).

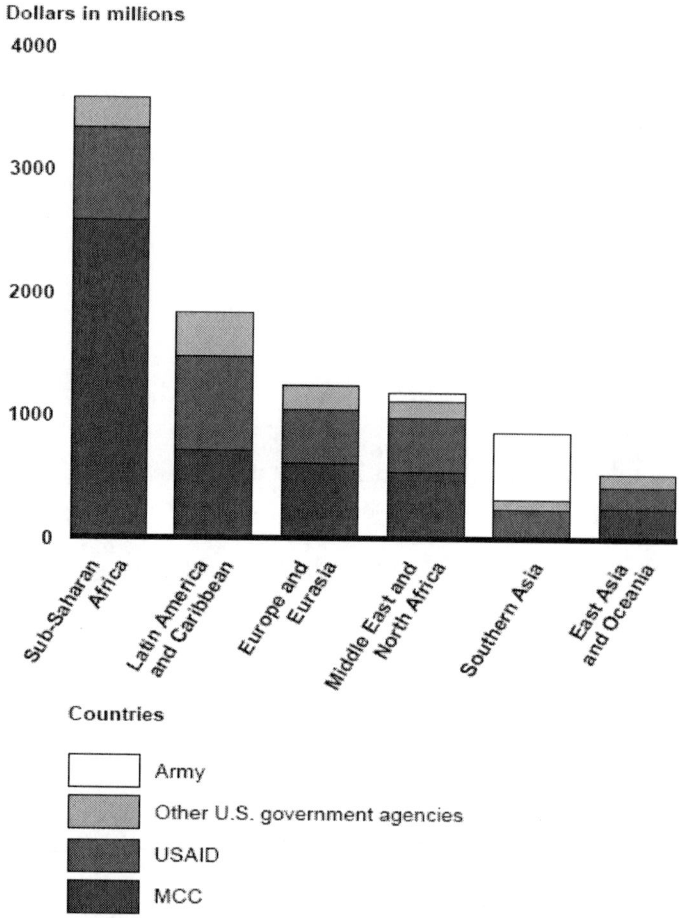

Source: GAO analysis of U.S. government TCB database.

Figure 4. Total U.S. TCB Funding by Agency and by Region, Fiscal Years 2005–2010.

Certain Factors Drive the Impact of MCC TCB Funding

The methodology of the TCB survey, the multiyear nature of MCC compacts, and the relatively large size of those compacts are factors that drive the impact of MCC funding on the TCB funding landscape. The TCB survey collects and reports funding for each fiscal year on an obligation basis, as opposed to reporting funding in the year in which it was distributed. MCC obligates full funding for its 5-year compact agreements in the year the compacts enter into force.[17] The TCB survey methodology captures the amount obligated in that year, resulting in large spikes in MCC annual figures. This is unique in that other U.S. agencies generally fund their multiyear projects through ongoing annual obligations. As a result, any comparisons between MCC funding and other agencies in any given year may be distorted. USAID officials noted that it may not be feasible to alter the data collection process in such a way as to address this issue.

As we have previously reported, MCC's actual disbursements have substantially lagged behind planned disbursements for countries with compacts in force.[18] This is because initial compact disbursement plans underestimated the time required for compact countries to establish the structures, agreements, and capabilities to begin implementing compact projects. For example, MCC signed a compact with Mozambique in fiscal year 2008 for $507 million and reported $222 million of that total as TCBrelated funding in that fiscal year. However, as of December 31, 2010, MCC reports having expended only $39 million, or just less than 8 percent of the total compact amount. Furthermore, due to the multiyear nature of MCC compacts, MCC funding usually constitutes a significant amount of total annual TCB funding, so the MCC obligations that appear in the TCB database are large relative to other agencies and have an increased impact on overall TCB statistics (see fig. 1).

USAID management officials acknowledge the potential for the database to distort the portrayal of TCB funding by comparing what is, in effect, 5- year funding for MCC with 1-year funding for other agencies, but they maintain that it is not possible to reconfigure the data in any meaningful way due to the survey's methodology. They also note that they sometimes remove MCC from the dataset when conducting their own analyses. In response to the concerns we noted, USAID updated the TCB Web site in July 2011 to include a prominent notice on the Web site's home page of the unique nature of MCC obligations. Given the relative size and impact of MCC funding, such explanation is necessary to fully understand the data.

The TCB Database Does Not Adequately Explain Significant Factors Driving Changes in the Composition of TCB Funding

The Database Does Not Fully Explain Limitations That May Cause Prior Years' Reporting to be Understated

Difficulties reporting previous years' data for newly identified sources of TCB funding may mean that funding levels for those years are understated in certain cases. The TCB survey team under contract with USAID annually reviews various sources, such as the President's budget request, to identify any TCB-related funding that is not currently being reported to the survey. In this way, the survey team identified the Army as a provider of TCB funding and requested that Army officials began submitting data beginning in 2009. The Army provided this funding for physical infrastructure development projects in Afghanistan and Iraq. The Army had provided funding for similar activities for a number of years prior; however, survey officials told us it was not practical to attempt to capture previous years' data. Although the TCB Web site notes that 2009 was the first year USAID received a submission from any of the U.S. Armed Services, it does not provide any further information. Specifically, it does not make users aware of the possibility that prior years' reporting is highly likely to be understated due to the challenges in reporting on the Army's previous funding. Furthermore, the TCB Web site does not note the process or describe the limitations of identifying new TCB funding sources in its methodology. The Army's funding made up 27 percent of the total TCB for 2009. Given the relative size and impact of Army funding, such an explanation is necessary to fully understand the data and the future impact of newly-identified agencies.

U.S. Agencies and Other Donors Sometimes Struggle to Determine the Extent of Trade-Related Investments

Reporting and measuring TCB-related funding and activities, particularly for physical infrastructure projects, can be difficult, largely because of the need to distinguish between assistance focused on improving trade capacity, in particular, and support to promote economic growth or some other goal in general. While agencies such as USAID fund activities that have clear and direct links to TCB, other agencies, including MCC and the Army, fund activities that are sometimes more indirectly related to international trade. For example, technical assistance USAID provides to aid in a country's accession to the WTO has a clear and direct relation to trade, but activities such as constructing roads or electrical grids may not. In addition, certain types of projects might be related to trade in one context but not in another. For instance, an energy project might relate to trade if it is servicing a tourism complex but not if it is providing electricity to local neighborhoods.

The TCB survey was developed to capture any and all U.S. government TCB-related funding at the activity level of all participating agencies. USAID and USTR officials have noted that the design of the TCB survey enables them to determine on a case-by-case basis the extent to which a project or program may relate to TCB because reporting officials understand the specific trade-related components of the project for which they are reporting data. USAID officials explained that the TCB survey is designed to solicit such a determination because it surveys those officials responsible for managing the projects "on the ground."

Although the TCB survey attempts to identify and quantify just the trade-related components of a physical infrastructure project, we found examples where the application of this distinction was challenging. Officials with whom we spoke during our fieldwork agreed that the definition of TCB used in the survey was quite broad, which could sometimes make it difficult to identify the activities to report in their survey responses. They relied on the categorical definitions provided by the TCB survey and survey guidance. However, we found instances in which officials experienced challenges in clearly discriminating between components of projects that were TCB or non-TCB related, particularly in large TCB-related infrastructure projects. For example:

- The Army reported $396 million in TCB funding for infrastructure projects in Afghanistan that consisted of activities intended to repair, restore, or build roads to respond to urgent humanitarian relief and reconstruction requirements and that also had trade-related effects. Army officials cited concerns about reporting the entire road project as related to TCB because it may only be minimally used for international trade. However, survey administrators advised Army officials responsible for reporting the Army's TCB data that the entire funding for the road project should be counted as TCB-related assistance "so long as the project is not designed to exclusively support a military installation and so long as the power/utility project is not designed to exclusively support residential use." As one official put it, "a road will support the ability of farmers to transport their products to a local market as well as to an export facility."

- In Morocco, MCC reported $116 million in TCB funding for a small-scale fisheries project in the physical infrastructure category. The activity is described in the TCB database in this way:

  "Fishing is one of the most important industries in Morocco. Morocco is unable to satisfy current domestic demand for quality fish. Demand is expected to increase, driven by an expanding tourist sector and expected growth in domestic fish consumption. The Small Scale Fisheries Project seeks to modernize the means of catching, storing, and marketing fish, thereby improving the quality of the catch, maintaining the value chain, and increasing fishers' access to both local and export markets."

  According to MCC and foreign officials in Morocco, external trade was not in the forefront of their thinking on this particular project when the compact was being developed. When we originally discussed this project with one MCC official in Morocco, we were told that 100 percent of the catch was intended for domestic consumption. However, we later learned from a host country project manager that an estimated 20 to 30 percent of the catch would go to outlets that might be considered exports. There was no readily available quantitative data to verify this. Differing from both those estimates, MCC had previously reported to the survey that all $116 million of funding for the project was TCB-related.

Other entities that report TCB-related funding face similar challenges. For example, the 2005 WTO Hong Kong Ministerial Conference established the Aid-for-Trade Initiative that prompted a joint effort by the OECD and the WTO to track TCB activities by all global donors in a manner similar to the approach of the TCB database. The U.S. TCB survey is used to generate the TCB activities and funding the U.S. government reports to that joint database. While the OECD and WTO effort collects and tracks aid-for-trade data using definitional categories similar to those used in the U.S. TCB survey, they more explicitly acknowledge the challenges associated with physical infrastructure projects. One OECD report notes that it is almost impossible to provide sound criteria that differentiate between trade-related infrastructure and general economic infrastructure. In addition, they report that few international donors can identify the trade-related share in individual projects and programs. As stated earlier in this report, USTR maintains that the U.S. TCB survey has the ability to determine on a case-by-case basis the extent to which projects may have trade-related components. USTR has explained that this ability to dissect programs into their component parts is an important difference between the U.S. TCB definition and OECD's aid-for-trade definition. However, we have noted examples when agency officials submitting TCB estimates have found it difficult to make this distinction.

USAID does not provide any information on the difficulties involved in making these determinations on the TCB database Web site. In contrast, the 2007 report on global aid-for-trade issued jointly by the OECD and the WTO[19] dedicates an appendix to discussing the difficulties in collecting data on infrastructure (as well as other categories of TCB) and the possibility that a significant over-estimation of the actual TCB-related volume is possible. The U.S. TCB survey attempts to make this differentiation but does not provide a clear explanation of how such a differentiation operates or the degree to which some of these determinations are subjective. Although the database states that the physical infrastructure category only includes assistance to establish telecoms, transport, ports, airports, power, water, and industrial zones that have a direct link to trade, it does not include a discussion of whether those projects are primarily for a non-TCB goal and how that might affect the project's value to TCB efforts.

Furthermore, the TCB database Web site does not distinguish or explain "direct" and "indirect" linkages between projects and TCB. USAID recognizes in its annual Congressional Budget Justification that there is a distinction between direct and indirect TCB. It cites examples of "direct TCB" that include support for countries' efforts to streamline customs and examples of "indirect TCB" that include modernizing transport. In neither of the examples above, where we noted instances in which officials experienced challenges in clearly discriminating between components of projects that were TCB or non-TCB related, was TCB explicitly the primary goal of the project. However, USAID officials provide no such distinctions or explanations on TCB database Web site, which could lead to users misunderstanding the data.

USAID Has Improved Its Assessment of TCB, but Has Not Made Plans to Make Use of Insights from a Recent Multicountry Evaluation, or to Conduct Additional Evaluations

USAID has made improvements in assessing the results of its TCB assistance, including developing indicators and taking the positive step of commissioning its first independent agencywide multicountry evaluation of TCB activities, as we recommended in our 2005 report.[20] The evaluation provided valuable information about the effectiveness of USAID's TCB assistance worldwide, and the factors associated with project success; however, the agency has yet to make specific plans to incorporate the evaluation's key insights into its planning and management of activities and conduct such evaluations in the future. To assess the immediate results of its TCB activities, USAID uses standard trade and investment indicators, and missions may develop additional custom indicators. In addition, it has commissioned a limited number of evaluations of specific TCB programs to assess longer-term results. However, most significantly, in 2010, USAID took the positive step of issuing an independent multicountry evaluation of U.S. government TCB assistance that focused on activities USAID administered. The evaluation provided the agency useful information on the effectiveness of USAID's activities across countries, the factors that influenced project success, and the means by which monitoring and evaluation could be improved. Although the agency is developing training based on the results of the evaluation, it has not developed plans for disseminating best practices to missions nor has it made plans for conducting such evaluations on an ongoing basis.

USAID Has Developed Indicators to Monitor Short-Term TCB Results, but Assessing Quality of Results Is Difficult

To assess and report on the immediate results of its TCB-related programs, USAID uses standard and custom indicators. (For further information on the frameworks agencies use for monitoring and evaluating their TCB activities, see app. V.) USAID requires missions to report performance against standard indicators, which include agencywide trade and investment indicators.[21] Activities in the trade and investment program area relate to TCB, and USAID uses 20 trade and investment standard indicators to measure the immediate results of its TCB activities.[22] Missions and offices report on a subset of the standard indicators that relate to the trade and investment program elements they are funding. Examples of USAID trade and investment standard indicators include:

- Number of customs harmonization procedures implemented in accordance with internationally accepted standards as a result of U.S. assistance.
- Number of investment measures made consistent with international investment agreements as a result of U.S. assistance.
- Reduction in the number of procedures required to trade goods across borders as a result of U.S. assistance.
- Number of firms receiving capacity building assistance to export.
- Number of participants in U.S. government-supported trade and investment capacity building trainings.
- Number of trade and investment capacity building diagnostics conducted.
- Number of U.S. government supported training events on topics related to investment capacity building and improving trade.

The standard indicators are complemented by custom indicators that USAID missions and offices select to further measure and monitor particular programs. USAID uses the indicators in performance plans and reports summarizing project results.

Some USAID officials noted that the standard indicators largely measure program outputs rather than results or outcomes of TCB assistance.[23]

Standard indicators generally gauge activities undertaken or services provided by USAID; for example, missions we visited used such output-oriented standard indicators as the number of U.S. government supported training events on topics related to investment capacity building and improving trade. However, they do not measure whether such activities contributed to a beneficiary country's capacity to trade. Our review of documentation of countries where USAID has conducted TCB activities revealed that these standard indicators serve certain USAID management purposes, but USAID mission officials told us it was difficult to use to such indicators to inform decisions about how TCB assistance could improve a country's capacity to trade. On the other hand, some USAID officials in recipient countries explained that in addition to the agencywide standard indicators, missions can develop project-specific custom indicators that tend to be more outcome-focused. For example, the mission in Morocco used the custom indicators, "total value of sales in target sectors (disaggregated by domestic sales and exports)" and "value of private investment (disaggregated by domestic and foreign direct investment)." Some program officers said that outcome-oriented custom indicators were more useful than the standard indicators for evaluating activities' effects on trade. Thus, based on data collected from a custom indicator that measured the volume of agricultural exports, program officials in Mozambique said that the mission modified the focus of an agriculture TCB-related program to target assistance to new crops with better export potential.

While the agency uses project-specific custom indicators for virtually every project, USAID management and mission officials cited challenges in developing meaningful outcome custom indicators. Some USAID officials explained that it is difficult to identify indicators that measure the effects of TCB directly attributable to U.S. government assistance. For example, one USAID official noted that many missions supporting TCB activities may track export growth as an outcome indicator, but according to mission officials, a variety of factors may impact a country's exports, including fluctuations in market prices and currencies, and it is difficult to isolate these factors from the effects of TCB assistance. Similarly, mission officials cited challenges to collecting and using valid and reliable data to gauge an indicator. For instance, in Mozambique, mission officials explained that local government trade data are not reliable, so they may have to rely solely on private sector data from firms targeted by the mission's TCB-related programs to measure exports. They said that this makes it difficult to compare the export performance of targeted beneficiary firms in the same sector. In addition, many USAID TCB-related activities are implemented as part of broader programs that have primary development objectives other than TCB. Consequently, the programs are assessed in relation to other objectives, and monitoring the effects on trade capacity may not be feasible if the performance indicators developed were not intended for that purpose.

USAID Has Commissioned a Limited Number of Evaluations of TCB Programs to Assess Longer-Term Results

USAID also commissioned longer-term evaluations of a small proportion of specific TCB programs. These include evaluations of its regional TCB-focused programs, including the Regional Trade Program for CAFTA-DR, the Andean Regional TCB Program, and the regional trade hubs in sub-Saharan Africa.[24] In addition, USAID has commissioned evaluations of its bilateral TCB programs, including the Colombia Trade Capacity Building Program implemented to support the U.S.-Colombia FTA negotiations.[25] The evaluations are intended to help missions and offices understand the progress of programs and any needed actions to improve performance. Although mission officials stated that evaluations are useful for identifying best practices and lessons learned, USAID's recent agencywide multicountry TCB evaluation found that only 15 percent of the agency's TCB projects were found to have been independently evaluated.[26] Mission officials informed us that they conduct few independent evaluations of their TCB programs because of the resources required, and the difficulty of evaluating impact in the area of TCB. In addition, they noted that program evaluations had not been required. According to USAID's 2010 evaluation guidance, missions are encouraged, but not required, to conduct program evaluations during implementation unless certain management issues arise.[27]

USAID's Recent Agencywide Multicountry Evaluation Provided Valuable Insights, but USAID Has Yet to Take Action to Address Results

To learn from experience and identify ways to improve the implementation and assessment of TCB activities, and in response to our 2005 recommendation, USAID took the positive step of commissioning its first independent multicountry evaluation of U.S. government TCB assistance that focused on activities USAID administered.[28] We support the evaluation as an important means of providing objective information on the progress of USAID's TCB efforts. It provided the agency valuable insights on the positive effects of USAID's TCB assistance across countries, particularly with regard to its impact on trade and income growth in recipient countries. It also provided useful information on the factors that contributed to and hindered project success, and the means by which monitoring and evaluation could be improved. Issued in November 2010, the evaluation examined documentation for 256 ongoing and completed USAID TCB projects the agency implemented in 78 countries from 2002 to 2006.

The Evaluation Identified Positive Effects of USAID's TCB Assistance

Overall, the evaluation concluded that USAID and other U.S. government agencies' TCB activities are associated with increases in the value of recipient countries' exports, after controlling for other factors that have influenced international trade. According to the evaluation's findings:

- USAID TCB activities had a positive effect on developing countries' exports, even in very poor countries, but the relationship between TCB assistance and export gains varied by country depending on factors that are known to influence export performance, including world prices and economic growth rates, and domestic economic and business policies.
- USAID's TCB activities resulted in export gains in terms of value, but not volume, which suggested that exporters earned more from the same volume of production they exported.
- Export gains associated with USAID's TCB projects stemmed from trade facilitation activities and from improvements in government practices, as well as from projects that work directly with exporters.
- USAID's TCB activities contributed to employment and income growth for those firms and individuals directly reached by USAID projects, although the evaluation did not find sufficient information on projects' effects on net employment or poverty rates at a regional or national level.

The Evaluation Identified Attributes that Are Associated with More Successful TCB Projects

The evaluation calls attention to characteristics that contributed to the success of USAID TCB projects and that tended to lead to sustainable outcomes. Some of these factors were associated with the focus of TCB assistance provided. For example, assistance that was directed at one type of beneficiary generally enjoyed better results than projects that included various categories of recipients. In addition, TCB projects that concentrated on a single sector generally performed better than projects that focused on multiple sectors. Thus, TCB projects that concentrated on the agricultural sector were more likely to successfully achieve their objectives than projects that attempted to cover diverse sectors, such as manufacturing and services, as well as agriculture. Conversely, projects that combined different types of assistance, such as performing a trade diagnostic study as well as providing training, were more likely to achieve their performance targets and objectives than projects that relied on a single approach. In some cases a combination of technical assistance, training and use of communications technologies helped change private sector practices, resulting in trade-related gains, such as new products for export and more timely delivery of goods.

The evaluation also describes certain factors related to beneficiaries' participation that were found to contribute to successful project results. For example, encouraging participation of beneficiaries in project design and promoting private sector involvement were also found to be associated with assistance efforts that met performance targets or objectives. Projects characterized by adversarial relations among participants were, however, less likely to succeed. Other factors that the evaluation cited as hindering project success included excessive host government regulation and unexpected shifts in the recipient government's priorities. The evaluation also found that improvements resulting from TCB assistance were more likely to be sustained beyond the life of the project when anticipated funding sources, such as revenues from export earnings, were clearly set forth.

The Evaluation Identified Weaknesses in USAID' s Efforts to Assess TCB Progress

Recognizing the importance of learning from experience and improving the implementation of TCB activities, USAID and USTR commissioned the evaluation to inform their efforts to develop an interagency strategy to systematically monitor results and evaluate the effectiveness of TCB assistance. Accordingly, the evaluation identified certain gaps in the monitoring and evaluation of TCB projects and recommended ways to improve USAID's performance management practices. The evaluation found that USAID's practices for monitoring the performance of its TCB projects does not correspond, in many instances, to the agency's performance guidelines, and its evaluations of TCB projects are limited in number and suffer from methodological weaknesses. For example:

- A large proportion of projects did not include baseline data for the performance indicators selected.
- While most projects identified performance indicators, most of these TCB projects did not include performance targets for the indicators to track results.
- While evaluations used both qualitative and quantitative data, most evaluations lacked data with which to compare circumstances before

and after TCB projects to determine whether the project's activities or some other factor were the likely cause of the results.

- Certain performance indicators intended to assess changes in institutional capacity, such as strengthening a given country's ministry of trade, lacked clarity in the outcome results they were designed to measure.

To improve USAID's monitoring and evaluation of its TCB projects, the evaluation recommended steps the agency should take to better align its performance management practices with its existing guidance. These include adopting tools to facilitate the development of appropriate indicators and data collection methods with which to measure results, and helping missions improve performance baseline data and targets for those projects that currently lack these data. In addition, the evaluation recommended that USAID update its current TCB strategy to better reflect findings from recent studies on trade facilitation and on other factors that influence developing countries' export performance.

USAID Has Yet to Take Action on the Evaluation's Results or Plan for Additional Evaluations

Although the evaluation examined the results of USAID's TCB activities for the purpose of learning from experiences, improving the design and implementation of TCB assistance, and informing efforts to systematically monitor and evaluate results, it has yet to take action to incorporate the results of the evaluation into its management of TCB activities. USAID management officials explained that the evaluation has been helpful in identifying the factors that contribute to the success of TCB projects and the agency agreed with the evaluation's findings and recommendations, particularly with regard to needed improvements in monitoring and evaluation practices. According to these officials, the agency has identified the need to incorporate the evaluation's findings into USAID's trainings, guidance, and strategies, as well as implement its recommendations, but further actions are needed to do so.

Officials explained that the written evaluation is lengthy, and technical officers managing TCB activities are not likely to easily understand its findings or find it useful for management purposes in its current form. USAID management officials stated that the evaluation's findings must be "repackaged" to help USAID missions and offices understand and use the information to improve the design, implementation, and the monitoring and evaluation of TCB activities. We have reported that performance information should be useful for decision making throughout an agency, and that agencies need to consider users' needs.[29] Currently, the agency is in the initial phases of developing ways to use the evaluation's findings to help missions develop better defined and more useful indicators, baselines, and targets with which to measure the results of TCB activities. For example, based on the results of the evaluation, USAID commissioned the development of a pilot training course on methods for developing outcome measures for monitoring and evaluating TCB programs. The pilot course provided an overview of the evaluation, described challenges of developing indicators to assess the outcome results of policy and institutional reforms on TCB, and discussed approaches to defining indicators and collecting measurements. The pilot course was presented to mission officials in Bangkok, Thailand, which one USAID management official explained had been a useful preliminary effort to incorporate the evaluation's findings into mission training. The official stated that a more comprehensive training program will likely be developed and disseminated to missions, although the agency has no specific plans in place. Differences in countries' trade and investment environments have proven a challenge to developing training and guidance that would be useful to missions worldwide, according to officials.

In addition, according to management officials, USAID has not determined its plans for conducting additional TCB evaluations to assess the effectiveness of its TCB activities on an ongoing basis. As the evaluation, published in November 2010, focused on TCB projects funded during the period 2002–2006, the agency does not have current plans to systematically evaluate its TCB projects worldwide and on an agencywide basis beyond this period. While USAID management officials stated that replicating the evaluation's methodology is likely to be too resource-intensive for future evaluations, any subsequent evaluations would similarly aim to assess a variety of TCB projects implemented across countries to identify those that are most successful in achieving their objectives and the factors that contribute to these successes. We have reported that it is important that agencies use timely performance information to assess the results of their activities to understand how they contribute to their agency missions and broader results.[30] Conducting evaluations on an ongoing basis increases accountability and would help ensure that assistance is effectively delivered and implemented to maximize development. It also would provide opportunities to learn from project implementation by identifying which activities work, under what circumstances, and why. For example, USAID officials could use future evaluations to identify approaches to providing TCB assistance that have worked well and consider alternative approaches where improvements could be made. Furthermore, such evaluations might inform other donor and recipient countries' efforts to determine instances in which TCB assistance can be effective.

CONCLUSION

The U.S. government and international organizations acknowledge the critical role of trade in promoting development and have made TCB an important aspect of making trade more effective in reducing poverty and increasing enduring economic growth. The U.S. government TCB database is a useful tool for identifying the many agencies and activities of the U.S. government that contribute to other nations' development through trade. In particular, the inclusion of MCC's funding and activities in the database creates opportunities to identify ways in which TCB funding and development goals relate. In addition, the Army's recent reporting highlights the linkage between security and development, as there is a recognition that economic stability and development contribute to peace and security. However, some U.S. agencies, including MCC and the Army, struggle to report their trade-related infrastructure assistance using the survey methodology of the database. The definition of TCB includes a wide array of activities implemented by multiple agencies to fulfill a variety of objectives. Some relate more directly to trade than others. While some agencies, such as USAID and State, conduct activities that are easily identified as intended to help a country build its capacity to trade, agencies such as MCC and the Army conduct activities that have trade-related effects but do not directly support TCB. This distinction has become increasingly important because of the significant funding reported by these two agencies, particularly for physical infrastructure, in USAID's TCB database. As a primary source of information on TCB funding for Congress and the public, it is important that its information create a clear picture of funding trends. But without explanations of the database's limitations, it may distort users' understanding and create misperceptions.

While USAID has taken positive steps to track the progress of individual TCB activities, like other development organizations it continues to struggle to link this assistance to important trade and development benefits. USAID's recent agencywide evaluation of the effectiveness of its TCB activities in multiple countries is an important step, but USAID officials have not yet signaled how they plan to address the evaluation's valuable findings. Without planning actions to utilize the results of its evaluation, the agency may miss opportunities to take advantage of the insights from that analysis to improve the effectiveness of its TCB assistance. Moreover, by evaluating its TCB activities across countries on an ongoing basis, USAID could gain a better understanding of the linkage between TCB and development. It could also gain valuable experience regarding the types of assistance important for the diverse set of countries and situations that could potentially benefit from U.S. TCB assistance.

Recommendations for Executive Action

To enhance the management and evaluation of TCB activities, we recommend that the Administrator of USAID take the following two actions:

- Explicitly and publicly report the identified limitations associated with the methodology used to collect and report data in the U.S. government TCB database, including MCC and the Army's data issues, and consider ways to differentiate between categories of assistance that directly and indirectly relate to TCB.
- Develop a written plan that details the actions the agency intends to take to address the findings and recommendations of its recent multicountry evaluation of TCB, and its plans for conducting evaluations of its TCB activities on an on-going basis.

Agency Comments and Our Evaluation

We received written comments from USAID. USAID stated that it has already taken steps consistent with our recommendations. USAID also noted that it would take our recommendations into account in its ongoing plans and provided additional information and observations.

USAID stated that it updated the TCB database to include fiscal year 2010 data and noted it had revised the Web site for the database to clarify the unique nature of MCC obligations. We believe this is a positive step, and will improve users' ability to accurately compare and assess data over time.

USAID further noted that it is reviewing its plans for the fiscal year 2011 survey of TCB activities and anticipates revamping and streamlining components of the database consistent with our recommendations. Clear reporting and transparency in methodology and collection are essential for users of the TCB database; the actions USAID has already taken, as well as those they state they intend to take, should facilitate the ability of users to understand changes in the nature of TCB over time.

Further, USAID noted it had recently completed a synopsis of the TCB evaluation which it is distributing to key stakeholders and other target audiences both within and outside the agency to highlight elements of the evaluation. In addition, USAID stated it is building on the pilot training of the evaluation's lessons, which we noted in the report, and is actively developing further training modules. However, at the time of our review USAID did not provide us with specific documentation of the actions it is planning to take to make use of the evaluation's findings and recommendations. Without developing a plan documenting specific actions the agency intends to take to utilize the results of its evaluation, the agency may not take full advantage of opportunities for improving the effectiveness of its TCB assistance identified in the TCB evaluation.

USAID also stated that under the agency's recently issued January 2011 evaluation policy, it is committed to a systematic monitoring and evaluation of USAID's entire portfolio of activities, including TCB activities, as the policy is fully implemented. While USAID's January 2011 evaluation policy encourages evaluations across the agency's portfolio of activities, the policy is not focused on TCB activities and does not specify the type of evaluation USAID will conduct on its TCB activities. We are suggesting that USAID document its specific plans for conducting TCB evaluations on an ongoing basis.

MCC, State, the Army, and USTR received a draft copy of the report but did not provide formal comments. State, USAID, and USTR provided technical comments, which we have incorporated in the report, as appropriate.

Loren Yager
Director,
International Affairs and Trade

APPENDIX I: OBJECTIVES, SCOPE, AND METHODOLOGY

This report examines (1) how agencies' trade capacity building (TCB) activities are aligned with the agencies' goals, (2) the extent to which the U.S. TCB database provides sufficient information on key trends and funding, and (3) the extent to which U.S. Agency for International Development (USAID) monitors and evaluates the effectiveness of its TCB activities. To address these objectives we built upon information collected for our 2005 report on the same topic. We conducted fieldwork in Colombia, Morocco, and Mozambique. We selected these countries because they (1) were among the 10 countries receiving the most TCB funding from fiscal years 2005 to 2009, (2) had a mix of U.S. agencies providing assistance and categories of TCB assistance provided in-country, and (3) had a diversity of geographic regions and country income levels. We limited our review to four agencies that provided more than 90 percent of total U.S. TCB assistance from fiscal years 2005 to 2010—the most recent fiscal year for which data are available. These include the Millennium Challenge Corporation (MCC), the Departments of the Army (Army) and State (State), and USAID. In addition, we included the Office of the U.S. Trade Representative (USTR) in our review due to its role in trade policy coordination.

To understand how agencies' TCB activities are aligned with the agencies' goals, we analyzed strategic, budget, and programmatic documents describing these agencies' TCB funding and activities. We assessed these agencies' reports and strategic plans to determine the extent they addressed agencies' TCB-related strategies and objectives. We examined U.S. government reports on TCB assistance, annual agency reports, and agency TCB planning and project documents. In each country we examined program documents and interviewed agency officials to understand the types of TCB programs the agencies managed. In conjunction with our work at the missions, we held meetings with other key U.S. government officials, USAID contractors, host government ministry officials, and various TCB recipients. To assess how U.S. agencies coordinate the allocation of TCB assistance, we reviewed published reports on TCB activities, agency strategies, and program documents. We interviewed U.S. officials in the field responsible for implementing TCB programs and officials at agency headquarters, including the USTR.

To describe the composition of TCB and determine the extent to which the TCB database provides sufficient information on key trends and funding, we analyzed available data on agencies' TCB activities and funding from the U.S.

government TCB database. USAID is responsible for maintaining the database and gathering data annually through a governmentwide survey. We analyzed data from the database to identify the major funding categories, agencies, and recipients of TCB assistance. As part of our previous and ongoing work, we have assessed this data and determined that they are sufficiently reliable to identify TCB funding by agency, country, and category; although we found limitations to the use of the data, as discussed in this report. We examined the guidance, protocols, and definitions specified in the TCB survey. We also reviewed documents from the Organization for Economic Cooperation and Development and the World Trade Organization (WTO) to understand definitions and data collection methodologies used globally for trade-related funding. In addition, we interviewed the USAID contractor that manages the data collection and analyzed the steps the contractor took to ensure data reliability. For example, we asked the contractor how the survey data were collected, what quality checks were performed, and what other internal controls were in place. At the missions overseas, we reviewed various TCB activities and interviewed U.S. and host country officials to corroborate the descriptions and funding levels reported in the TCB database.

To understand the extent to which USAID monitors and evaluates the effectiveness of their TCB activities, we analyzed strategic, budget, and programmatic documents describing these agencies' TCB funding and activities. We reviewed data and information these agencies use to measure the performance of their activities, and, where available, evaluations of programs or projects they undertake that may be related to TCB. In particular, we reviewed a recent USAID evaluation study, commissioned in response to our previous recommendations and intended to present findings of a cross-country evaluation of U.S. government TCB assistance. In each country we visited we reviewed agencies' strategy documents and performance plans and reports for activities reported as TCB. We also interviewed agency officials, host government officials, and contracted implementing partners and visited TCB projects. In addition, we examined performance and monitoring principles used by multilateral donors and international organizations, such as the Organization for Economic Cooperation and Development.

We conducted this performance audit from July 2010 through July 2011 in accordance with generally accepted auditing standards. Those standards require that we plan and perform the audit to obtain sufficient, appropriate evidence to provide a reasonable basis for our findings and conclusions based on our audit objectives. We believe that the evidence obtained provides a reasonable basis for our findings and conclusions based on our audit objectives.

APPENDIX II: USAID PLANS TRADE CAPACITY BUILDING-RELATED ACTIVITIES IN-COUNTRY, OFTEN IN COLLABORATION WITH RECIPIENT GOVERNMENTS AND STAKEHOLDERS

USAID field missions plan TCB-related projects primarily in recipient countries, often in collaboration with recipient country governments and other in-country stakeholders. USAID's TCB strategy recognizes that priorities vary from country to country depending on the levels of income and development, and the missions' country strategic plans and resources will inform the selection and prioritization of the TCB activities the agency implements. According to USAID officials, mission officials understand country-specific factors such as the activities of other TCB donors and the composition of trade. The USAID officials informed us that missions identify their TCB projects as part of their mission strategic plans, which USAID's headquarters bureaus review in conjunction with the agency's budget planning process. They further explained that USAID's headquarters bureaus provide missions guidance and training, and help missions develop and design specific programs when necessary; however missions primarily identify the country-specific trade-related constraints and TCB assistance needs in consultation with governments and associations in recipient countries. In addition, missions use trade diagnostic studies and analyses of trade-related constraints and TCB needs.

According to USAID officials, missions plan TCB activities using analyses of trade-related constraints and TCB-related needs prepared by the recipient government and in-country stakeholders, including business and trade associations. For example, specific activities of the USAID TCB programs related to the U.S.-Colombia free trade agreement (FTA) negotiations responded to priorities defined in collaboration between USAID and the government of Colombia as the negotiations were carried out. Specifically, USAID officials stated that they collaborated with the government of Colombia to identify 52 TCB initiatives. Following the completion of the FTA negotiations in 2006, USAID continued to provide technical assistance to support the initiatives, and by 2010 the mission had addressed all but two of these initiatives. According to mission officials, the mission in Mozambique identified TCB activities, in part, based on the country's trade association's evaluation of trade-related constraints. Mission officials cited the importance of involving the business association and various government ministries to identify feasible policy reforms and foster the collaboration. For example, the mission has worked with the business association and the Ministry of Commerce to reduce import and export barriers, and reform licensing and shipment processes. In addition, these officials explained that they have daily interactions with officials of various ministries and these discussions will often identify potential areas for TCB assistance.

USAID missions also use trade diagnostic studies sponsored by USAID and developed by multilateral agencies to identify trade-related constraints and TCB needs. According to mission officials in Colombia and Mozambique, these diagnostic studies are important to encourage recipient governments to undertake needed reforms. For example, USAID commissioned three diagnostic studies to identify and plan TCB assistance in support of the U.S.-Colombia FTA negotiations. Based on study results, USAID developed seminars to increase awareness of both the Colombian congress and civil society about the importance of the FTA and how regions and productive sectors would benefit from it. In Mozambique, multilateral and bilateral stakeholders developed a diagnostic study that mission officials said contributed to the mission's decisions regarding sectors and areas of the country where it provided technical assistance under its TCB-related agribusiness and tourism programs. For example, according to mission officials, the study contributed to the agribusiness program's focus on commodities such as cashews and coconuts from the country's northern region that have the greatest export potential. Furthermore, according to one government of Mozambique official, the mission utilized the study results to encourage the government to develop a national strategy to address trade-related constraints to economic growth.

We also found that USAID missions generally select TCB-related activities that align with broader country development strategies. In countries we visited, mission officials cited the importance of consulting with recipient governments' national development strategies and with foreign officials of recipient countries to identify potential TCB-related activities that have the support of the recipient governments. For example, the mission in Mozambique identified TCB-related activities under its agribusiness and policy reform programs that directly supported the implementation of priorities identified in national strategies of various ministries. In Morocco, the mission supported the government of Morocco's strategy of providing jobs, economic opportunities, and political stability through free trade. The mission identified the potential economic challenges posed by the FTA, particularly in the area of agriculture, and outlined activities to help the government of Morocco respond to the challenges and opportunities posed by the FTA. According to mission officials, the mission worked with Moroccan associations to promote transparent and simplified investment procedures, increase access to finance for small businesses, and increase assistance to the Ministry of Agriculture to promote a shift in the country's agricultural production to higher value crops.

APPENDIX III: COORDINATION OF U.S. TRADE CAPACITY BUILDING ASSISTANCE AMONG AGENCIES

USTR leads efforts to coordinate the TCB activities of USAID and other U.S. agencies through interagency groups and committees tied to FTAs and in response to multilateral initiatives related to TCB. USTR-led interagency groups often seek U.S. agencies' input into TCB-related issues and identify the types of assistance agencies have provided and may be able to provide in a particular area. In addition, U.S. agencies coordinate their TCB-related activities in recipient countries as part of interagency groups that discuss general development assistance activities, but which do not focus on TCB specifically. For example, USAID coordinates its TCB-related activities with other U.S. agencies in-country, as appropriate, through embassy-led task forces and working groups focused on development assistance in the area of economic growth. These interagency groups seek to prioritize projects with broader foreign assistance strategies, eliminate duplication of efforts, and identify where assistance gaps exist, for instance.

USTR Leads Efforts to Coordinate U.S. TCB Assistance among U.S. Agencies

USTR leads efforts to coordinate the TCB activities of USAID and other U.S. agencies through interagency groups and committees tied to FTAs. USTR has created TCB interagency groups in free trade negotiations with developing countries and committees on TCB to prioritize and coordinate TCB activities to help FTA partner countries participate in negotiations and implement trade rules during the transition and implementation periods. Interagency groups have been a feature of the FTAs with Bahrain, Central America-Dominican Republic, Chile, Jordan, Morocco, Oman, and Peru. According to USTR officials, these interagency groups do not influence the outcomes of FTA negotiations; however, interagency groups and committees meet periodically in conjunction with ongoing and completed negotiations to discuss partner countries' TCB needs, determine the types of TCB activities agencies already provide, and identify the types of TCB assistance agencies might provide in the future. According to USTR officials, the interagency groups tied to the FTAs offer USTR the opportunity to work with other agencies to try to identify the types of assistance they may be able to provide in a particular area. USAID and other U.S. agencies participate in these working groups and committees so that identified TCB needs are incorporated into ongoing assistance programs. For example, according to USTR officials, during a 2008 meeting of the Central America-Dominican Republic FTA TCB Committee, agencies identified sanitary and phytosanitary assistance as a priority, and with USDA assistance, each partner country's sanitary and phytosanitary system was assessed and gaps or deficiencies in those systems were identified. In response, State, USAID, USDA, and USTR reached agreement to provide further sanitary and phytosanitary assistance. In addition, in 2010, USAID, U.S. Customs and Border Protection, and USTR developed training sessions in all Central America-Dominican Republic FTA partner countries to address textiles compliance issues the interagency committee had identified, according to USTR officials.

USTR also leads the coordination of agencies' TCB-related activities resulting from Trade and Investment Framework Agreements (TIFA) between the United States and partner countries.[1] According to USTR officials, USTR works with other agencies—including the U.S. Patent and Trademark Office and the Departments of Commerce, Justice, and State—in working groups that respond to partner countries' assistance needs and priorities. TIFAs also prompt regular meetings between the U.S. government and the partner country. Officials explained that these discussions are led by USTR for the United States, but a number of other agencies also participate and TCB is often a part of these dialogues. For example, officials noted that USTR recently chaired a meeting with the government of Mauritius in which the Department of Commerce presented TCB tools and trainings that it provides. Similar meetings with South Africa and Nigeria have also included representatives from a number of different agencies and included TCB discussions.

In addition, USTR coordinates TCB efforts with USAID and other agencies through the Trade Policy Staff Committee (TPSC) and its associated subcommittees.[2] Following the Hong Kong WTO Ministerial in 2005, the U.S. administration formed a TPSC Subcommittee on TCB. According to officials, the subcommittee has focused on WTO developments in the area, including USTR's sharing of information regarding the WTO and other multilateral initiatives related to TCB, such as the Enhanced Integrated Framework,[3] and seeking other agencies' input. As these initiatives had near- and long-term implications for the WTO, a permanent subcommittee of the TPSC was deemed the appropriate mechanism for interagency coordination, according to USTR officials. All members of the TPSC are invited to participate in meetings of the TPSC Subcommittee on TCB. In addition, other agencies that have a particular interest or expertise in TCB assistance are also invited, including MCC. USTR utilizes other TPSC subcommittees to coordinate U.S. agencies' TCB efforts in various contexts. For example, the TPSC Subcommittee on Africa has discussed TCB issues particularly related to the African Growth and Opportunity Act, and the TPSC Subcommittee on Labor has discussed TCB issues related to FTA labor commitments and trade preference program labor obligations.

U.S. Agencies Coordinate TCB Activities in-Country As Part of Interagency Groups Focused on Broader Assistance Objectives

U.S. agencies generally coordinate their TCB-related activities in-country, primarily through mechanisms that do not focus on TCB, but which discuss TCB-related assistance in connection to broader foreign assistance objectives. In conducting our fieldwork we found that embassy-led task forces and working groups sometimes discuss agencies' TCB-related activities, as appropriate. For example, according to officials in Morocco, USAID, State, MCC, and other agencies discuss their TCB-related activities as part of the embassy's foreign assistance working group that aims to prioritize projects in alignment with broader foreign assistance strategies, eliminate duplication of efforts, and identify where assistance gaps exist. Through Ambassador-led working group meetings and communications with headquarters in Washington, D.C., agencies have identified and coordinated their specific TCB-related activities, such as USAID and State's collaboration on activities that promote access to finance, and USAID's focus on working with the government of Morocco to promote policy reforms, particularly in support of MCC's projects. In Mozambique, the mission coordinates TCB-related activities through the embassy's private sector working group that focuses on foreign assistance covering multiple economic sectors, according to officials. Officials noted that the working group has reviewed the mission's TCB-related agricultural development projects in conjunction with similar projects conducted by other agencies. In particular, through the working group mission officials have worked regularly with USDA officials to coordinate the processing and storage of agricultural production supported by each agency's TCB-related projects.

APPENDIX IV: RECIPIENT COUNTRIES OF BILATERAL U.S. TRADE CAPACITY BUILDING ASSISTANCE AND FUNDING LEVELS, FISCAL YEARS 2005–2010

Table 2 shows the 143 countries that received roughly $8.5 billion in bilateral TCB funding between fiscal years 2005 and 2010. Of the 20 countries receiving the largest obligations, all but 5—Afghanistan, Colombia, Sudan, Iraq, and Egypt—are MCC compact countries. These 20 countries received $6.3 billion, or 74 percent, of total U.S. TCB assistance over the period. Among these 20 countries, 8 are least developed countries (LDC) according to the definition used by the United Nations. In total, 43 LDCs received $3.6 billion or 43 percent of total bilateral TCB funding. Of the four agencies we reviewed, MCC obligated the most funding, $2.3 billion, to LDCs, while USAID obligated $618 million, the Army obligated $550 million, and State obligated $8 million. Figure 5 illustrates the shares of TCB funding obligated to LDCs in total and for each agency.

Table 2. Countries Receiving TCB Funding Obligations, Fiscal Years 2005–2010

Country (by amount of funding)	Total TCB funding (fiscal years 2005–2010)	Least developed country	MCC recipient country
Afghanistan	758,936,000	*	
Tanzania	606,139,000	*	*

Country (by amount of funding)	Total TCB funding (fiscal years 2005–2010)	Least developed country	MCC recipient country
Morocco	577,406,000		*
Senegal	507,002,000	*	*
El Salvador	452,537,000		*
Burkina Faso	398,015,000	*	*
Georgia	323,600,000		*
Ghana	292,134,000		*
Colombia	284,558,000		
Moldova	263,643,000		*
Mozambique	258,409,000	*	*
Honduras	229,999,000		*
Mongolia	198,548,000		*
Iraq	196,702,000		
Benin	188,979,000	*	*
Nicaragua	175,040,000		*
Egypt	169,551,000		
Mali	159,492,000	*	*
Armenia	121,630,000		*
Sudan	120,771,000	*	
Lesotho	102,085,000	*	*
Jordan	95,027,000		*
Cape Verde	87,318,000	*	*
Namibia	85,173,000		*
Ukraine	77,672,000		*
Indonesia	76,174,000		
Bolivia	74,146,000		
West Bank/Gaza	73,905,000		
Peru	69,972,000		
Dominican Republic	69,140,000		
Madagascar	66,658,000	*	*
Ethiopia	61,662,000	*	
Philippines	60,875,000		*
Vanuatu	54,525,000	*	*
Guatemala	53,474,000		
Liberia	49,195,000	*	*
Kazakhstan	46,206,000		

Table 2. (Continued)

Country (by amount of funding)	Total TCB funding (fiscal years 2005–2010)	Least developed country	MCC recipient country
Serbia	38,850,000		
Vietnam	37,847,000		
Macedonia	37,363,000		
Ecuador	37,252,000		
India	36,641,000		
Uganda	36,328,000	*	
Romania	33,804,000		
Pakistan	33,718,000		
Rwanda	33,603,000	*	
Hungary	32,332,000		
Paraguay	32,257,000		*
Mexico	31,735,000		
Kyrgyzstan	29,338,000		
Cambodia	28,859,000	*	
South Africa	28,845,000		
Nigeria	27,038,000		
Kenya	26,922,000		
Azerbaijan	24,040,000		
China (P.R.C.)	22,210,000		
Zambia	21,141,000	*	*
Tajikistan	20,207,000		
Bosnia and Herzegovina	20,137,000		
Russia	18,781,000		
Haiti	18,635,000	*	
Brazil	17,399,000		
Croatia	16,961,000		
Thailand	16,133,000		
Timor Leste	15,258,000	*	
Guyana	15,234,000		*
Malawi	14,853,000	*	
Albania	12,902,000		
Serbia and Montenegro (FRY)	12,306,000		

Table 2. (Continued)

Country (by amount of funding)	Total TCB funding (fiscal years 2005–2010)	Least developed country	MCC recipient country
Belarus	1,266,000		
Papua New Guinea	1,157,000		
Cote dIvoire	1,105,000		
Maldives	971,000	*	
Latvia	840,000		
Cameroon	818,000		
Mauritius	813,000		
Chad	667,000	*	
Slovak Republic	646,000		
Guinea-Bissau	600,000	*	
Uruguay	599,000		
Bahrain	580,000		
Poland	472,000		
Trinidad and Tobago	461,000		
Dominica	446,000		
Gambia	417,000	*	
Barbados	404,000		
Libya	337,000		
Gabon	292,000		
Qatar	272,000		
Korea, Rep.	200,000		
Zimbabwe	195,000		
St. Lucia	173,000		
Bahamas	114,000		
St. Kitts and Nevis	80,000		
St. Vincent and Grenadines	69,000		
Solomon Islands	60,000	*	
Seychelles	51,000		
Fiji	43,000		
Belize	38,000		
Sierra Leone	26,000	*	
Suriname	23,000		
Swaziland	23,000		

Country (by amount of funding)	Total TCB funding (fiscal years 2005–2010)	Least developed country
Lebanon	11,640,000	
Uzbekistan	11,149,000	
Turkmenistan	10,574,000	
Angola	10,178,000	*
Nepal	9,904,000	*
Kosovo	9,773,000	
Costa Rica	9,228,000	
Democratic Republic of Congo (Kinshasa)	8,620,000	*
Yemen	8,438,000	*
Sri Lanka	8,278,000	
Bangladesh	7,926,000	*
Montenegro	7,880,000	
Togo	7,864,000	*
Algeria	6,796,000	
Turkey	6,527,000	
Guinea	6,149,000	*
Chile	5,589,000	
Oman	5,575,000	
Central African Republic	5,400,000	*
Jamaica	5,127,000	
Malaysia	5,088,000	
Laos	4,859,000	*
Sao Tome and Principe	4,000,000	*
Argentina	3,927,000	
Burundi	3,862,000	*
Panama	3,703,000	
Bulgaria	3,100,000	
Cyprus	2,928,000	
Botswana	2,015,000	
Djibouti	2,000,000	*
Tunisia	1,809,000	
Lithuania	1,383,000	
Niger	1,374,000	*

Country (by amount of funding)	Total TCB funding (fiscal years 2005–2010)	Least developed country	MCC recipient country
Bhutan	21,000	*	
Venezuela	20,000		
Micronesia (Fed States)	16,000		
Mauritania	14,000	*	
Tonga	13,000		
Congo (Brazzaville)	11,000		
Samoa	11,000	*	
Grenada	5,000		

Source: U.S. government TCB database.

Note: Many U.S. government departments and agencies fund and implement TCB activities that cannot be disaggregated by country, but are regional or global in scope. The obligations in this table were on a bilateral basis and do not include amounts obligated regionally or multilaterally.

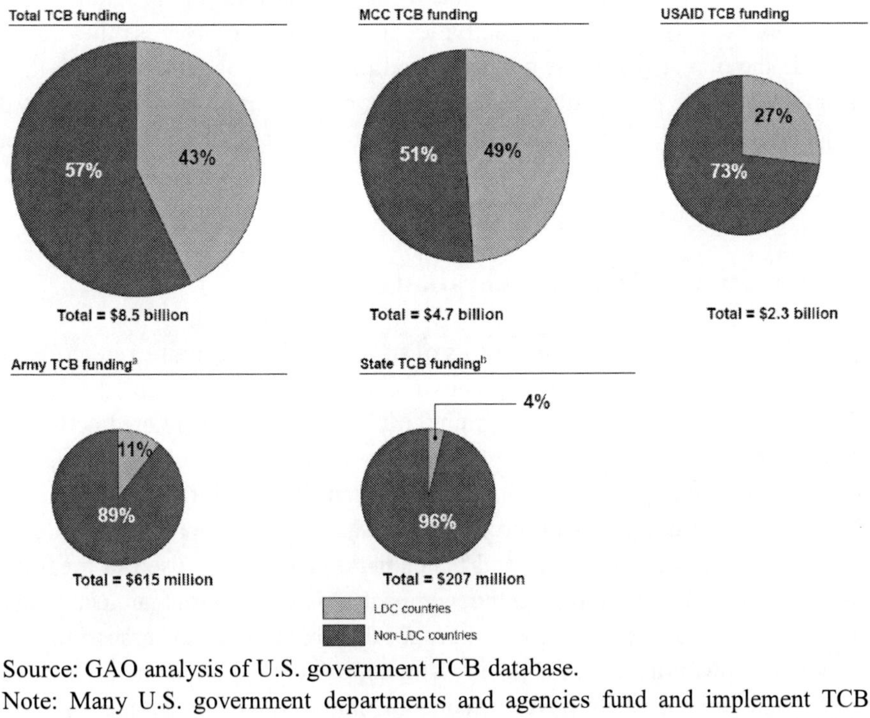

Source: GAO analysis of U.S. government TCB database.

Note: Many U.S. government departments and agencies fund and implement TCB activities that cannot be disaggregated by country, but are regional or global in scope. The obligations in this table were on a bilateral basis and do not include amounts obligated regionally or multilaterally.

[a]The Army reported TCB funding for only three countries, with the bulk of funding going to Afghanistan, an LDC.

[b]The majority of TCB reported by State was regional or global in scope which is not represented in these bilateral figures.

Figure 5. Share of Bilateral Obligated TCB Funding by LDC Status, Fiscal Years 2005–2010.

APPENDIX V: MCC AND THE ARMY ASSESSMENTS OF TRADE CAPACITY BUILDING-RELATED ACTIVITIES

MCC and the Army do not use TCB-specific performance indicators and evaluations to assess the progress of their activities in terms of TCB. Each agency uses its overall monitoring and evaluation framework to assess their TCB-related activities in relation to the agency's missions and program goals. MCC monitors its TCB-related activities in terms of the progress they make towards the objectives of the compacts and threshold programs in which they are included. The procedures the Army uses to assess individual TCB-related projects are based on the types of project funding and the primary project objectives.

Millennium Challenge Corporation

MCC does not monitor the results of its TCB-related activities in terms of TCB, but monitors progress using its overall policies for monitoring the results of its compacts and threshold programs. MCC monitors TCBrelated activities in terms of their progress towards the immediate results and final program objectives of the compacts and threshold programs in which they are included. During compact development, project appraisals and development procedures include defining the objectives and benchmarks that will be used to measure progress over the duration of the compact. MCC performs an economic analysis on each compact project proposal, which includes assessing the economic growth rationale for the investment, calculating an economic rate of return, and estimating its poverty reduction impacts. The economic analysis results in the indicators MCC uses to monitor its compact projects, including those that it reports as TCB.[1] Project managers may monitor additional indicators for their own management purposes. While the economic analysis and the selection of additional indicators may result in indicators meaningful to measure the effects of activities on trade, MCC does not identify a particular set of TCB-specific performance indicators to monitor TCBrelated compact projects in terms of their effectiveness in building the trade capacity of the compact country. Similarly, the indicators used to monitor TCB-related activities included in threshold programs are not specific to TCB, but are identified during program development. The selection of performance indicators for threshold programs are based on information on the policies and actions that may have affected the threshold country's standing in relation to the MCC's eligibility criteria.

In the two compact countries we visited—Morocco and Mozambique—most projects MCC reported as related to TCB were not assessed using performance indicators meaningful for measuring progress in terms of TCB, according to in-country MCC officials. These officials explained that projects MCC reported as TCB could have been assessed using trade-related indicators, such as the volume and value of exports stemming from projects, because they have trade-related effects. However, these officials explained the economic analysis of the compact projects and the project manager's selection of additional indicators did not result in indicators that directly measured the results of projects in terms of trade. For example, in Morocco, officials noted that the performance indicators used to monitor three TCB-related compact projects did not provide information to track results in terms TCB, but monitored projects' effects on household incomes and employment. Similarly, in Mozambique, none of the three compact projects MCC reported as TCB-related were monitored in terms of their effects on trade, according to in-country officials. Although these officials explained that all three projects result in trade-related outcomes, including a road rehabilitation project that facilitates the transport of goods for export and an agriculture development project that resulted in production for export, the projects were monitored in terms of other objectives. For example, the objectives of a TCB-related roads rehabilitation project in the Mozambique compact included reduced transport costs, and increased public transport access for individuals to take advantage of job and other economic opportunities. The economic analysis of the project focused on the reduction of transport costs, including savings in vehicle operating costs, and time savings. Examples of performance indicators for the project included measures of the roughness of the road and the dollar value of time saved due to shorter trip times and increased speed on upgraded roads.

In addition, MCC conducts independent evaluations of its compacts and threshold programs to better understand the effectiveness of its development programs; however, these evaluations are not intended to directly evaluate projects in terms of TCB. According to MCC's monitoring and evaluation policy, every compact project and each threshold program must undergo a comprehensive, independent evaluation after completion, and compact projects may be evaluated during compact implementation as necessary. The evaluations are intended to compile lessons learned and improve the effectiveness and efficiency of project implementation. Evaluations also are meant to compare projects' final results with a credible estimate of what would have happened without the project, including changes in individual, household, or community income that result from a particular project or program. According to MCC officials in the countries we visited, evaluations had not yet been conducted on compact projects, including TCB-related projects, but each project would be evaluated upon the completion of the compact. These officials explained that the evaluation will be conducted in accordance with agency guidance to assess the performance of specific activities and contribute to a broader understanding of development effectiveness. While the evaluation may assess the trade-related results of projects as trade may contribute to the economic growth and poverty reduction objectives of the compact, officials explained that an assessment of the effectiveness of compact projects in terms of TCB would not be a specific focus.

The Department of the Army

The Army does not have a specific process for monitoring and evaluating the performance of projects reported as TCB, but uses its general guidance and processes for assessing projects. According to officials of one command, the infrastructure projects identified as TCB are not monitored using performance indicators specific to TCB, and the Army does not evaluate the effectiveness of its TCB-related infrastructure projects in terms of TCB. Officials explained that the monitoring and evaluation procedures used to assess individual TCB-related projects depend on the types of funding used for specific projects and the project's primary objectives. For example, according to officials, TCB-related projects funded under the Commander's Emergency Response Program (CERP), which include TCB-related projects implemented to respond to humanitarian and reconstruction requirements in Afghanistan, are monitored and evaluated using processes outlined in CERP guidance, which do not include methods for monitoring and evaluating projects' effects on trade. TCB-related projects funded under CERP include the repair and restoration of telecommunications and electrical systems, and irrigation projects. According to the July 2009 CERP guidance, performance indicators for CERP projects are selected based on each project's scope, complexity, and period of usefulness. In identifying procedures for evaluating projects, officials are to consider certain factors, including the benefits of the project to the local population, and the number of individuals in the local population engaged in and benefiting from the project; also the project must meet engineering standards.

End Notes

[1] GAO, Foreign Assistance: U.S. Trade Capacity Building Extensive, but Its Effectiveness Has Yet To Be Evaluated, GAO-05-150 (Washington, D.C.: Feb. 11, 2005).

[2] In January 2004, Congress established MCC to administer the Millennium Challenge Account for foreign assistance.

[3] The WTO has no formal definition of a "developing country." Members announce for themselves whether they are "developed" or "developing" countries.

[4] WTO agreements contain special provisions that give developed countries the possibility to treat developing countries more favorably than other WTO members. These special provisions include, for example, longer time periods for implementing agreements and commitments or measures to increase trading opportunities for developing countries. The provisions are designed to help developing countries implement the agreements and to accentuate the benefits they might enjoy.

[5] USTR uses the term "aid for trade" interchangeably with TCB.

[6] USAID, USAID Strategy: Building Trade Capacity in the Developing World, PD-ABX-241 (Washington, D.C., March 2003).

[7] The program's 18 components included (1) seminars on the FTA and its benefits, (2) labor capacity and compliance with labor laws and regulations, (3) customs reforms, (4) technical barriers to trade, (5) tax benchmarking, (6) securities market, (7) investment, (8) modeling of demand for transportation infrastructure, (9) sanitary and phytosanitary measures, (10) tax policy, (11) telecommunications, (12) technical cooperation strategy to build trade capacity and harmonize donor assistance, (13) services statistics, (14) professional services standards, (15) competitiveness, (16) arbitration, (17) intellectual property rights, and (18) energy sector.

[8] Sanitary refers to human and animal health and safety, while phytosanitary refers to plant health.

[9] Countries include Afghanistan, Azerbaijan, Ethiopia, Kazakhstan, Kyrgyzstan, Laos, Russia, Serbia, and Tajikistan.

[10] Also knows as the Agreement on Trade Related Aspects of Intellectual Property Rights.

[11] The 15 member countries of the Southern African Development Community (SADC) region launched a free trade area in 2008. In addition, SADC member states have begun negotiations to form a Tripartite FTA combining SADC, the Common Market for Eastern and Southern Africa, and the East African Community.

[12] Pub. L. No. 106-200, Title I, 114 Stat. 252 (2000), as amended. AGOA requires the administration to produce an annual report on the U.S. trade and investment policy for sub-Saharan Africa and the implementation of AGOA. The report includes information about TCB efforts undertaken by U.S. agencies in the region, including USAID.

[13] A compact is a multiyear agreement between the MCC and an eligible country to fund specific programs targeted at reducing poverty and stimulating economic growth. A threshold program is designed to assist countries that have not yet qualified for MCC compact funding, but are on the "threshold" of doing so, having demonstrated a significant commitment to improving their performance on the eligibility criteria for compact funding. See 22 USC 7708 (a), (j).

[14] Compact countries include Armenia, Benin, Burkina Faso, Cape Verde, El Salvador, Georgia, Ghana, Honduras, Lesotho, Madagascar, Mali, Moldova, Mongolia, Morocco, Mozambique, Namibia, Nicaragua, Senegal, Tanzania, and Vanuatu. Threshold countries include Guyana, Jordan, Liberia, Moldova, Paraguay, the Philippines, Sao Tome and Principe, Ukraine, and Zambia.

[15] The objective of the Commander's Emergency Response Program (CERP) is to enable local commanders in Iraq and Afghanistan to respond to urgent humanitarian relief and reconstruction requirements within their areas of responsibility. The Secretary of the Army serves as the executive agent and is responsible for developing detailed procedures necessary for commanders to carry out CERP in a manner that is consistent with applicable laws, regulations, and guidance. The Commander of U.S. Central Command is responsible for allocating CERP resources. CERP guidance applies to all U.S. Department of Defense organizations and activities.

[16] For the purposes of analysis, we grouped the TCB categories used by the survey, and listed in table 1 in the background, into the following eight groupings: (1) physical infrastructure development; (2) trade facilitation; (3) WTO-related (includes WTO awareness and accession and WTO agreements); (4) governance, transparency and interagency coordination; (5) human resources and labor standards; (6) financial sector development and good governance; (7) trade-related agricultural development; and (8) other TCB categories (includes environmental sector trade and standards, competition policy and foreign investment, and services trade development including tourism)..

[17] The Millennium Challenge Act of 2003 (Pub. L. No.108-199, Div. D, Title VI, Sec. 605) authorizes MCC to provide assistance to countries that enter into public compacts with the United States. MCC has negotiated compacts with countries that contain agreed upon assistance objectives, responsibilities, implementation schedules, expected results, and evaluation strategies. The act stipulates that a compact may not last longer than 5 years and that MCC may have only one compact with a country at a time.

[18] GAO, Millennium Challenge Corporation: Analysis of Compact Development and Future Obligations and Current Disbursements of Compact Assistance, GAO-08-577R (Washington, D.C.: Apr. 11, 2008).

[19] Organization for Economic Development and World Trade Organization, Aid for Trade At A Glance 2007: 1st Global Review.

[20] GAO-05-150.

[21] State and USAID developed the standard indicators in 2006 as part of the State and USAID joint strategic framework to measure the results of U.S. government foreign assistance funding and the impact of efforts to advance countries' development. They are intended to facilitate the aggregate reporting of quantitative information across countries.

[22] State divides standard indicators USAID uses into three categories, (1) strategic level, designed to capture the impact of foreign and host-government efforts at the objective level; (2) program area level, intended to measure results beyond what could be achieved solely by U.S. government-funded interventions; and (3) element level, designed to measure outputs that are directly attributable to the U.S. government's programs, projects and activities.

[23] Output measures are the direct products and services delivered by a program. Outcome measures are the results of products and services provided.

[24] Chemonics International, Inc., USAID Regional Trade Capacity Building Program for CAFTA-DR: Final Report (August 2010); Nathan Associates, Inc., USAID Andean Regional Trade Capacity Building Program: Final Report, October 1, 2005 to June 19, 2006 (June 2006); DAI/Nathan Group, African Trade Hub Best Practices Review: Building on Successes and Lessons Learned for the Next Generation of Trade Hub, (July 2010); and Global Business Solutions Inc., Evaluation of Trade Hubs Located in Accra, Ghana; Gaborone, Botswana, and Nairobi, Kenya: Final Report (August 2006).

[25] Trade Services Group, Colombia Trade Capacity Building Support Project Final Report: December 2004 to December 2006 (December 2006).

[26] Molly Hageboeck, Management Systems International, From Aid to Trade: Delivering Results: A Cross-Country Evaluation of USAID Trade Capacity Building (November 2004).

[27] In January 2011, USAID issued a new evaluation policy. The policy requires that all major programs be evaluated at least once and that an evaluation include its methodology and plans for dissemination. In addition, the evaluation must be timed so that the findings will be available as decisions are made about new strategies, program designs, and procurements. Recognizing the need for the funding of evaluations, the policy suggests that at least 3 percent of program funds be used for commissioned independent evaluations.

[28] Management Systems International, From Aid to Trade: Delivering Results, A Cross-Country Evaluation of USAID Trade Capacity Building (November 2010).

[29] GAO, Results-Oriented Government: GPRA Has Established a Solid Foundation for Achieving Greater Results, GAO-04-38 (Washington, D.C.: Mar. 10, 2004).

[30] GAO, Managing for Results: Enhancing Agency Use of Performance Information for Management Decision Making, GAO-05-927 (Washington, D.C.: Sep. 9, 2005).

End Notes for Appendix III

[1] TIFAs provide strategic frameworks and principles for dialogue on trade and investment issues between the United States and the other parties to the TIFA. These agreements serve as a forum for the United States and other governments to meet and discuss issues of mutual interest with the objective of improving cooperation and enhancing opportunities for trade and investment.

[2] The TPSC is chaired by USTR and composed of 20 federal agencies and offices. It seeks to develop and coordinate U.S. government positions on international trade and trade-related investment issues. Supporting the TPSC are more than 90 subcommittees responsible for specialized areas and several task forces that work on particular issues.

[3] The Enhanced Integrated Framework for Trade-Related Assistance to Least-developed Countries is a program comprised of multiple organizations and donors that operates as a coordination mechanism for trade-related assistance to least-developed countries (LDC). The program assists LDCs incorporate trade into national development strategies, establish structures needed to coordinate the delivery of trade-related technical assistance, and address trade-related constraints. Its members include the WTO, World Bank, the International Monetary Fund, United Nations Conference on Trade and Development, United Nations Development Program, and the International Trade Centre.

End Note for Appendix V

[1] After a compact is signed, the partner country's accountable entity and MCC finalize a monitoring and evaluation plan that lays out the framework for monitoring and evaluating compact activities and the process for assessing progress towards the compact goal. The plan identifies the indicators, performance targets, and details for collecting data and reporting progress against performance targets.

In: Trade Capacity Building
Editor: Richard T. Royce
ISBN: 978-1-63463-733-6

Chapter 2

FOREIGN ASSISTANCE: USAID SHOULD UPDATE ITS TRADE CAPACITY BUILDING STRATEGY*

United States Government Accountability Office

ABBREVIATIONS

CDCS	Country Development Cooperation Strategy
FTA	free trade agreement
MCC	Millennium Challenge Corporation
OPIC	Overseas Private Investment Corporation
State	Department of State
TCB	trade capacity building
TPSC	Trade Policy Staff Committee
USAID	U.S. Agency for International Development
USTR	Office of the U.S. Trade Representative
WTO	World Trade Organization

* This is an edited, reformatted and augmented version of a Congressional Research Service publication GAO-14-602, prepared for Members and Committees of Congress, dated August 2014.

WHY GAO DID THIS STUDY

Since at least 2001, the United States has provided TCB assistance to developing countries to help them participate in and benefit from global trade. Multiple agencies provide this assistance, which may include support for World Trade Organization accession, customs procedures improvement, or development of infrastructure such as ports and roads. In this report, GAO focuses primarily on USAID because it provided the most funding for TCB in fiscal year 2012 and has a formal strategy focused entirely on TCB. GAO was asked to review the strategy, which is more than a decade old. GAO was also asked to examine USAID efforts to coordinate TCB activities to ensure that the United States is fulfilling its commitment in the most effective way.

In this report, GAO (1) determines the extent to which USAID's 2003 strategy guides USAID's TCB activities and (2) describes methods USAID uses to coordinate TCB efforts with other U.S. government agencies at home and abroad. GAO analyzed agency documents, interviewed relevant officials, and conducted fieldwork in six countries in Africa and Asia, selected for their diverse stages of development and geographic locations.

WHAT GAO RECOMMENDS

GAO recommends that the Administrator of USAID update the 2003 TCB strategy to reflect the current TCB environment. USAID agreed with the recommendation.

WHAT GAO FOUND

The U.S. Agency for International Development's (USAID) 2003 trade capacity building (TCB) strategy does not directly guide TCB activities, and parts of the strategy no longer reflect the current TCB environment. USAID's TCB activities are primarily guided by country needs and many of these activities are elements of large development projects that have their own objectives. According to USAID, the strategy's priority areas—participation in trade negotiations, implementation of trade agreements, and economic responsiveness to opportunities for trade—remain relevant. However, some parts of the strategy are not current. For example, the strategy does not include discussion of how USAID should coordinate with the Millennium Challenge Corporation (MCC), which did not exist in 2003 and is a major TCB contributor (see figure). USAID officials told GAO that they had not updated the strategy because they questioned the costs and benefits of doing so given that trade resources were declining and they believed the priorities presented in the strategy were still relevant. However, USAID is still committing significant resources to TCB, and TCB contributes to goals outlined in USAID and the Department of State's joint strategic plan. USAID's TCB strategy may not be as useful as it could be for informing TCB activities because parts of it are no longer current. Moreover, directives, such as those in the Government Performance and Results Act Modernization Act of 2010, can serve as guidance for periodic updating of strategic plans.

U.S. Government Trade Capacity Building Related Obligations by Agency, Fiscal Year 2012 (U.S. dollars in millions)

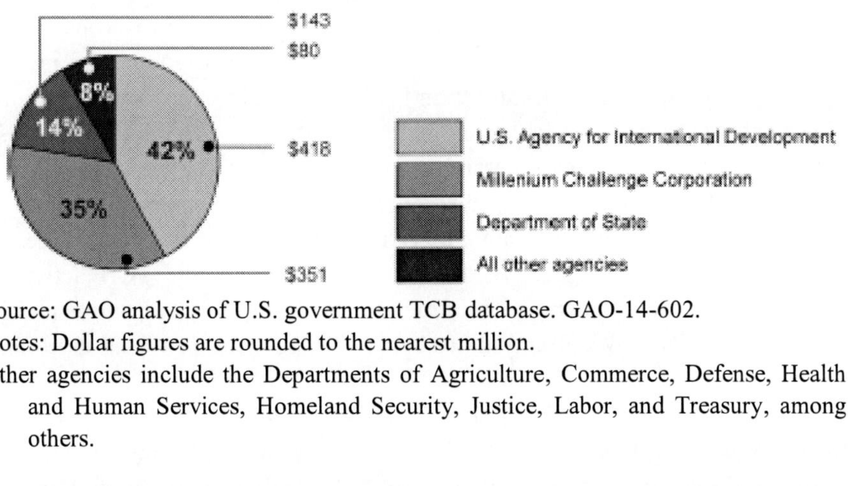

Source: GAO analysis of U.S. government TCB database. GAO-14-602.

Notes: Dollar figures are rounded to the nearest million.

Other agencies include the Departments of Agriculture, Commerce, Defense, Health and Human Services, Homeland Security, Justice, Labor, and Treasury, among others.

The 2003 strategy calls for USAID to be the primary coordinator for U.S. government TCB efforts, and GAO found that USAID coordinates TCB activities at home and abroad using a range of methods, including structured and informal dialogue between stakeholders. Specifically, USAID staff report that they participate in interagency working groups and maintain ongoing discussions with counterparts from other agencies to coordinate TCB activities. For example, at headquarters USAID participates in the Trade Policy Staff Committee, an interagency working group that includes a range of stakeholders and has subcommittees on development and TCB. In the countries GAO visited, GAO found that USAID missions coordinate TCB through formal mechanisms, such as working groups, as well as informal communication.

* * *

August 11, 2014

The Honorable Bob Corker
Ranking Member
Committee on Foreign Relations
United States Senate

Dear Senator Corker:

Since at least 2001, the United States has been committed to providing trade capacity building (TCB) assistance to developing countries to help them participate in and benefit from global trade. TCB assistance may include support for World Trade Organization (WTO) accession, customs procedures improvement, or development of infrastructure such as ports and roads. TCB covers multiple categories of assistance across numerous types of trade and development programs that have many goals and are implemented by multiple agencies. Given the diffused nature of TCB assistance, Congress has expressed concern about which agency is ultimately accountable for TCB activities. While the U.S. government is committed to providing TCB, no single agency is responsible for it. We found in 2011 that U.S. agencies provided more than $9 billion in TCB assistance from 2005 through 2010, based on data from the U.S. government TCB database, administered by the U.S. Agency for International Development (USAID).[1] In fiscal year 2012, U.S. government agencies provided nearly $1 billion for TCB activities in more than 120 countries, customs territories, and regional groupings. Given the diverse and disparate nature of TCB activities, congressional oversight of key aspects of this effort, including strategy, coordination, and program management, is important to ensuring that the U.S. government is meeting its TCB commitment. In this report, we focus primarily on USAID because it is the agency that provided the most funding for TCB—about $418 million—in fiscal year 2012, and has a strategy focused entirely on TCB, released in

2003.[2] In addition, the strategy calls for USAID to take a primary role in coordinating TCB assistance.

You expressed an interest in the current status of USAID's TCB strategy, which is more than a decade old. In addition, you asked us to gain a better understanding of USAID efforts to coordinate TCB activities and to use evaluations to manage them, to help ensure that the United States is fulfilling its TCB commitment in the most effective way. In this report, we (1) determine the extent to which USAID's 2003 strategy guides USAID's TCB activities; (2) describe methods USAID uses to coordinate TCB efforts with other U.S. government agencies at home and abroad; and (3) describe how, if at all, USAID has used TCB evaluations in its program and project management. You also asked us for information on USAID's and the Department of State's (State) obligations and appropriations accounts for TCB efforts. We identified, for fiscal years 2011 and 2012, the appropriation accounts from which USAID and State allocated funds for TCB-related activities and the obligations from these accounts for such activities and provided this information to you in a February 2014 briefing (see app. I).

To address these objectives, we built upon information collected for our 2005 and 2011 reports on TCB and analyzed data from the U.S. government TCB database.[3] Data from the TCB database were previously deemed reliable for our 2005 and 2011 reports on TCB. We identified limitations to the TCB database in our 2011 report on TCB, including that the database did not adequately explain significant factors driving changes in the composition of TCB funding over time. For this report, we assessed data from fiscal years 2008 through 2012 and determined that the data were sufficiently reliable to identify TCB funding by agency, country, and category. Furthermore, in assessing the data, we interviewed key USAID officials and the contractor responsible for administering the database and reviewed supporting documentation.

We primarily focused on TCB activities that USAID conducted because USAID provided the most funding of all U.S. agencies for TCB activities in 2012. However, we also sought the views of three other entities in our review regarding coordination with USAID on TCB activities: (1) State, because it is committed to supporting the negotiation and implementation of trade agreements and thereby helps countries advance trade initiatives; (2) the Millennium Challenge Corporation (MCC) because it conducts TCB-related activities that support its broader strategic and agency mission goals, although it does not have a specific TCB mission; and (3) the Office of the U.S. Trade Representative (USTR) because of its role in leading trade efforts. In conducting our work, we analyzed strategic, budget, and programmatic documents describing these agencies' TCB funding and activities. We also reviewed evaluations of TCB projects. We conducted fieldwork in Vietnam, Laos, Thailand, Ethiopia, Tanzania, and Kenya. We selected these countries because they (1) had a cross-section of projects that would allow us to compare and contrast different types of activities, (2) are at different stages of economic development, (3) are in diverse geographic regions, or (4) had signed an MCC compact and received MCC-related TCB assistance. In each country, we analyzed agencies' strategy, coordination, and program management efforts. We also interviewed agency officials, host government officials, and contractors implementing TCB activities in the field and visited TCB project sites. Our findings from these countries are not generalizable to the universe of all USAID TCB activities. Appendix II provides a detailed discussion of our objectives, scope, and methodology.

We conducted this performance audit from October 2013 to August 2014 in accordance with generally accepted government auditing standards. Those standards require that we plan and perform the audit to obtain sufficient, appropriate evidence to provide a reasonable basis for our findings and conclusions based on our audit objectives. We believe that the evidence obtained provides a reasonable basis for our findings and conclusions based on our audit objectives.

BACKGROUND

Definition and Goal of Trade Capacity Building

TCB is usually defined broadly to include all types of development assistance that positively affect a country's ability to secure benefits from international trade. Such assistance includes addressing

- the regulatory environment for business, trade, and investment;
- constraints such as low capacity for production and entrepreneurship; and
- inadequate physical infrastructure, such as poor transport and storage facilities. (See app. III for a detailed list of TCB category definitions in the U.S. government TCB database.)

USAID's TCB goal is to increase the number of developing countries that are harnessing global economic forces to accelerate growth and increase incomes.

Roles of Key Agencies Involved in TCB

A variety of U.S. agencies have a role in providing TCB assistance. In fiscal year 2012, according to the U.S. government TCB database, a total of 19 organizations obligated funding for TCB-related activities.[4] The roles and responsibilities of four key agencies involved are described below:

- *USAID*: One of USAID's core development objectives is to promote sustainable, broad-based economic growth by helping developing countries increase their exports through trade capacity building. As outlined in its March 2003 document, *Building Trade Capacity in the Developing World*, USAID aims to achieve its TCB goal by supporting participation in trade negotiations, implementation of trade agreements, and economic responsiveness to trade opportunities. USAID plans, funds, and implements TCB activities at both the agency and country levels. According to USAID's 2003 TCB strategy, USAID should take a primary role in coordinating assistance among agencies engaged in TCB activities. In fiscal year 2012, USAID obligated about $418 million for TCB-related activities worldwide.
- *State*: Under its strategic goal of promoting economic growth and prosperity, State has committed to supporting the negotiation and implementation of trade agreements. State's Trade Policy and Programs staff help countries advance global, regional, and bilateral trade initiatives, including free trade agreements (FTA) and World Trade Organization (WTO) initiatives. In fiscal year 2012, State obligated about $143 million for TCB-related activities worldwide.
- *MCC*: As we reported in 2011, MCC conducts TCB-related activities—mostly associated with infrastructure development—that support its broader strategic and agency mission goals. However, MCC does not have a specific TCB mission or strategic plans and goals relating specifically to TCB. In fiscal year 2012, MCC obligated about $351 million for TCB-related activities worldwide.

- *USTR*: USTR does not implement or fund any TCB programs but leads trade negotiations that may create demand for TCB assistance or may result in agreements that create opportunities for TCB to improve the ability of the recipient to benefit from its provisions. USTR also plays an advisory role to agencies with programmatic responsibilities, informing those agencies about TCB needs or opportunities related to trade initiatives or negotiations and needs that might emerge related to USTR's broader responsibilities for U.S. international trade policy.

Sixteen other organizations also obligated about $80 million in TCB-related assistance in fiscal year 2012. See figure 1 for illustrative examples of TCB activities that agencies conducted in the countries we visited during our fieldwork.

USAID Obligated the Most Funds for TCB-Related Activities of Any Agency in Fiscal Years 2011 and 2012

For the two most recent years for which data are available (fiscal years 2011 and 2012), USAID TCB-related obligations totaled more than $1 billion, making USAID the agency that contributed the largest amount during that period. Some obligations reflect agencies' provision of infrastructure and development projects that had trade-related effects— and were therefore counted as TCB—but were conducted to fulfill broader objectives. For example, while USAID reported more than $1 billion in TCB-related obligations for fiscal years 2011 through 2012, the trade and investment program area of USAID's budget for those years consisted of a total of about $348 million.[5]

Over the past 5 years, USAID, State, and MCC provided a total of about $6.7 billion in TCB-related assistance (see fig. 2).

USAID's TCB Strategy

In 2003, USAID issued a formal strategic plan on TCB—*Building Trade Capacity in the Developing World*—to focus its TCB efforts and guide the selection of new activities.

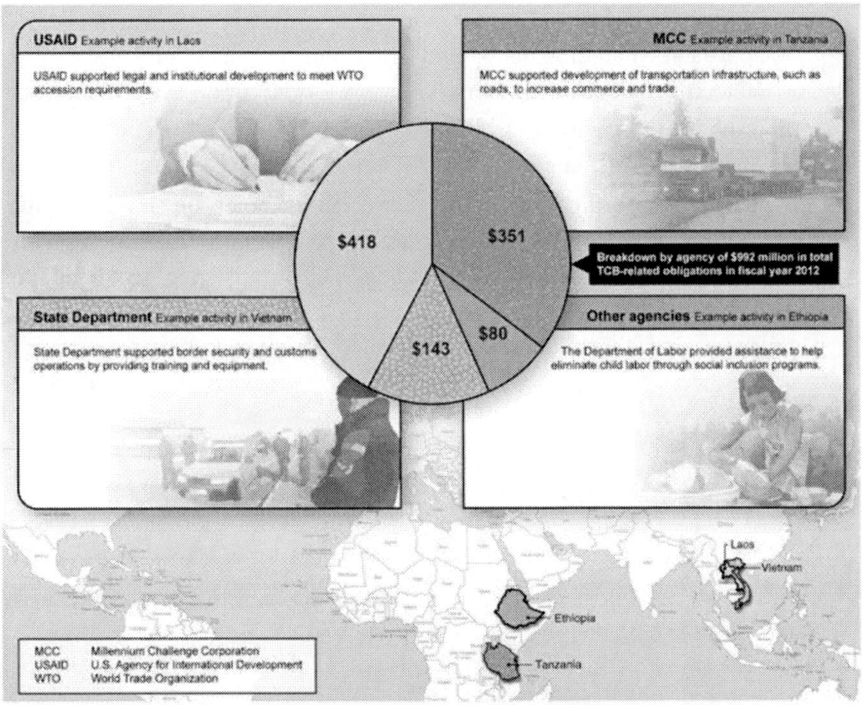

Source: GAO analysis of agency documents and U.S. government TCB database (data). Map resources (map). GAO-14-602.

Notes: Dollar figures are rounded to the nearest million. Other agencies include the Departments of Agriculture, Commerce, Defense, Health and Human Services, Homeland Security, Justice, Labor, and Treasury, among others.

Figure 1. Multiple Agencies Provide Trade Capacity Building (TCB) Related Assistance through a Broad Range of Activities Worldwide.

The plan calls for USAID's TCB projects to support the three priority areas of helping countries participate in trade negotiations, implement trade agreements, and take advantage of trade opportunities.[6] The strategy was developed partly in response to the Doha Development Agenda and U.S. commitments to increase global economic growth through free markets and free trade, according to USAID officials.[7] Among other things, the strategy

- defines overall TCB priorities and includes discussion of agency-wide and country-level TCB strategies;

- discusses specific considerations that influence the agency's TCB approach, including labor and environment issues, and negotiations concerning trade agreements;
- provides information on TCB categories and definitions and USAID's TCB initiatives; and
- discusses coordination with other U.S. agencies on TCB activities, calling for USAID to take a primary role in coordination assistance among all the agencies providing TCB assistance to developing countries.

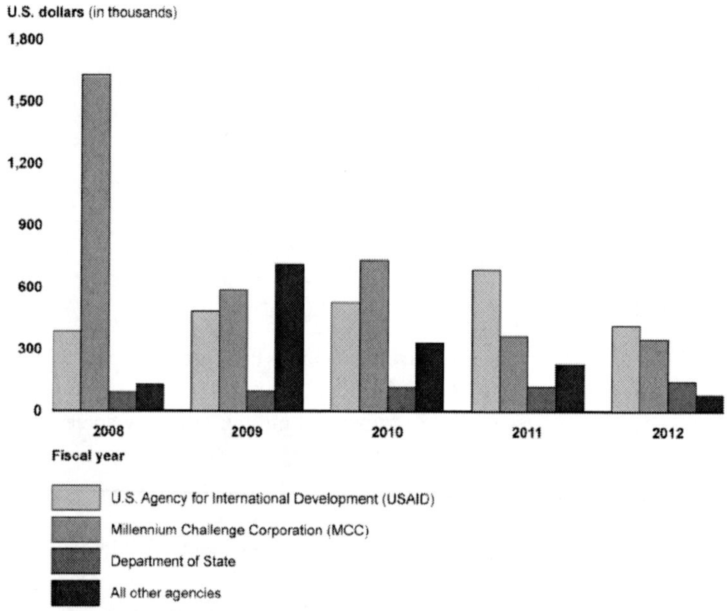

Source: GAO analysis of U.S. government TCB database. GAO-14-602.

Notes: Comparisons between MCC and other agencies' funding in any given year may appear distorted because MCC obligates full funding for its 5-year compact agreements in the year the compacts enter into force. The TCB survey methodology captures the amount obligated in the single year the compact enters into force, resulting in large spikes in MCC annual figures for certain years. For more information, see GAO-11-727.

Depending on the specific fiscal year, other agencies may include the Departments of Agriculture, Commerce, Defense, Health and Human Services, Homeland Security, Justice, Labor, and Treasury, among others.

Figure 2. Obligations for Trade Capacity Building (TCB) Related Activities by Agency for Fiscal Years 2008 through 2012.

Among the four key agencies that we reviewed, USAID is the only one that has issued a formal strategy focused entirely on TCB.

Prior GAO Work on TCB

In response to continued congressional interest in oversight, we undertook reviews of U.S. TCB activities and issued reports in 2005 and 2011. In our 2005 report, we recommended that USTR and USAID develop a cost-effective strategy to monitor and measure program results and to evaluate the effectiveness of U.S. TCB assistance. In response, USAID in consultation with USTR developed a multicountry evaluation to measure the effectiveness of U.S. TCB assistance that was issued in November 2010. In our 2011 report, we recommended that the Administrator of USAID publicly report identified limitations and key distinctions in the definitional categories of TCB assistance in the U.S. government TCB database. (For more information about the TCB database and definitional categories, see app. III.) Beginning in 2011, USAID streamlined and clarified the definitions of TCB categories to facilitate reporting and improve transparency. This change was reflected in the "technical notes" section of the TCB database.

USAID's TCB Strategy Does Not Guide TCB Activities and Parts of It Are No Longer Current

TCB Activities in the Field Are Guided by Country-Specific Needs

According to USAID officials, development and implementation of TCB activities in the field are guided more by country-specific strategies that incorporate country needs, circumstances, and priorities than by USAID's 2003 TCB strategy. This approach is consistent with guidance provided by the TCB strategy, as well. Specifically, USAID's TCB strategy states that the selection and prioritization of TCB activities at the country level will continue to be determined by missions' country-specific strategic plans and resources. USAID officials also stated that in countries associated with specific trade negotiations or agreements, TCB activities are also derived from the needs identified through those negotiations or agreements.

The main strategy document that guides USAID activities in the field, including TCB activities, is the missions' Country Development Cooperation Strategy (CDCS), according to USAID officials. USAID policy requires most USAID missions to prepare a CDCS, which is a 5-year strategy that serves as the basis for the mission's assistance planning, budgeting, and resource allocation and is based on country needs and U.S. priorities. It is developed in consultation with partner country governments and citizens, civil society organizations, the private sector, multilateral organizations, other donors, and other USG agencies. USAID officials at the USAID Mission in Ethiopia stated that the mission's CDCS is the main strategy guiding their TCB activities. For example, Ethiopia's CDCS calls for TCB-related activities under its objective of increasing economic growth with resiliency in rural Ethiopia. This objective focuses on strengthening agricultural value chains—the process or activities by which relevant firms add value to a product—by increasing the availability of market-based information, among other things. The objective also focuses on improving private sector competitiveness through efforts such as trade and customs reform. The Agribusiness and Market Development Project is an example of TCB activities in Ethiopia that were guided by this objective. The Agribusiness and Market Development project has activities aimed at improving the global competitiveness of selected value chains for products such as sesame, chickpeas, and coffee, and increasing private sector access to finance and investment.

To help identify TCB needs and provide further strategic guidance for their development of specific TCB programs, USAID missions also use ongoing trade negotiations—such as bilateral trade agreements or World Trade Organization (WTO) accession—and commitments made under existing trade agreements. During our fieldwork, USAID officials in both Vietnam and Laos reported that development and implementation of the mission's TCB activities were guided by needs identified by USAID and the host government during the negotiation and implementation of trade agreements and WTO accession. Specific examples of TCB assistance that was guided by these events are Vietnam's Support for Trade Acceleration Projects (STAR I and STAR II), which ran from 2001-2010. STAR I and II provided technical assistance to the Vietnamese government to facilitate revision of its commercial laws, legal procedures, transparency, and appeals processes to meet requirements under the U.S. and Vietnam bilateral trade agreement and the WTO.

Many TCB Activities Are Components of Large Development Projects That May Not Have TCB as a Primary Objective

According to USAID officials, a large portion of the agency's TCB assistance is provided as a component of large development programs with their own strategies, goals, and objectives. These large programs provide TCB as a means to achieving other development objectives, such as food security, adaptation to climate change, or democracy and governance, and are therefore guided by strategies and policies directed at those objectives. We found examples of such programs in the African countries we visited, Tanzania and Ethiopia. USAID's officials in the East Africa and Tanzania missions reported that most of the TCB-related activities in Tanzania are part of the "Feed the Future" initiative and are therefore guided by USAID's Feed the Future strategy for the country.[8] An example of such activities is the Staples Value Chain Development project in Tanzania. This project includes activities aimed at improving the competitiveness and productivity of maize and rice value chains in Tanzania, and facilitating improved domestic and regional trade.[9] This activity is guided by the Feed the Future Strategy but also clearly facilitates trade and thus has TCB components.

A USAID official reported that because TCB assistance is often a component of large development programs, USAID's total reported TCB assistance deliberately includes a broad range of activities to capture all types of U.S.-provided TCB assistance. The official stated that a large portion of USAID's total reported TCB assistance is for non-TCB focused development projects that have TCB-related effects. USAID officials reported that in some cases TCB needs to be woven into other development projects as there is no dedicated funding source for TCB activities. For example, USAID mission officials in Ethiopia reported that they work TCB into broader agriculture and other development programs because they have no dedicated funding for specific TCB programs.

USAID's 2003 TCB Strategy Identifies Priorities for TCB Activities but Does Not Reflect the Current TCB Environment

The 2003 TCB strategy identifies priorities for TCB that USAID officials told us are still relevant but does not reflect changes in the TCB environment that have occurred over the past decade.[10] The strategy, while not directive, is intended to provide guidance, context, and options to help operating units understand their specific roles related to TCB, according to USAID officials. For example, agency-level strategies, such as the TCB strategy, should be incorporated into missions' CDCS, according to USAID guidance on mission-specific strategies. According to USAID officials, the priorities presented in the TCB strategy—participation in trade negotiations, implementation of trade agreements, and economic responsiveness to opportunities for trade— are still relevant and cover all TCB activities although the strategy has not been updated since 2003. USAID officials also noted that the strategy is supplemented with guidance related to specific TCB activities and trade agreements. However, since the strategy was developed, the TCB environment in which USAID operates has changed significantly. For example, the total number of free trade agreements the United States has entered into has increased from 3 in 2003 to 14 as of May 2014, and the number of trade and investment framework agreements signed by the United States increased from 19 in 2003 to 50 as of May 2014. In addition, according to USAID, most of the developing countries it has worked with have become WTO members.

It is generally accepted that strategies should be periodically updated to reflect the current environment. For example, according to USAID's guidance, its mission country development cooperation strategies are only 5-year strategies. We also note that the Government Performance and Results Act Modernization Act of 2010 requires agencies to update and revise their strategic plans at least every 4 years.[11] In addition, desirable characteristics of a national strategy include discussion of the current operating environment.[12] Moreover, a multicountry evaluation of USAID's TCB assistance, released in 2010, stated that the usefulness of USAID's 2003 TCB strategy diminishes as time passes and the base of empirical literature on TCB and U.S. development policy evolves.[13] The evaluation recommended that USAID update the 2003 strategy to reflect the latest developments and findings on trade facilitation and other determinants of developing country export performance.[14]

Given the changes that have occurred over the past 11 years, USAID's 2003 TCB strategy is outdated in several areas. For example,

- *The coordination section of the strategy does not include all agencies now providing TCB assistance.* The number of agencies involved in providing TCB increased from 15 in 2003 to 19 in 2012, but the coordination section of the strategy does not reflect that change. For example, the strategy does not discuss how USAID is to coordinate with MCC, the second-largest contributor of TCB assistance in fiscal year 2012, since MCC was established after 2003.

- *Some trade initiatives discussed in the strategy are no longer current.* The strategy refers to a number of outdated initiatives, including the proposed Free Trade Area of the Americas, for which negotiations ended in 2005 with no agreement. It also refers to a number of potential trade agreements that have since been completed, including the Dominican Republic-Central American Free Trade Agreement and the U.S.–Morocco Free Trade Area.
- *The strategy does not reflect changes in emphasis placed on TCB priorities.* Changes since 2003 in the emphasis, or importance, USAID places on each priority are not reflected in the strategy. For example, USAID reported that it has placed more emphasis recently on trade facilitation initiatives, such as streamlining customs clearance procedures and increasing transparency. USAID has also reported utilizing fewer resources on the priority of participation in trade negotiations in recent years, conducting fewer activities related to WTO accession because many of the developing countries USAID has worked with have become WTO members.
- *The TCB database categories of TCB activities, included as an appendix to the strategy, have changed.* The original list of categories of TCB activities provided in the strategy's appendix no longer match up exactly with the current database categories that USAID uses. USAID streamlined the categories in fiscal year 2011, resulting in fewer overall.
- *The strategy does not incorporate lessons learned from over 10 years of TCB assistance.* For example, the strategy does not reflect changes in USAID's approaches to providing TCB assistance since 2003, and it does not include lessons learned identified in the 2010 multicountry evaluation of TCB assistance.

USAID officials in Washington, D.C., told us that although they have had discussions about updating the strategy, they have not updated it because they question the costs and benefits of a new strategy given that trade resources are declining and because the priorities presented in the strategy still remain relevant, in their view. A USAID official reported that the focus in recent years had been on supporting ongoing field programs and that these efforts took precedence over updating the TCB strategy. USAID officials also reported that they believe an update to the existing strategy would have limited impact, largely serving to maintain the status quo, since the priorities have remained the same and all activities still fit under the strategy. However, we previously found that assessing the current environment has a critical impact on the success of strategic planning.[15] Further, even though USAID reports that trade resources are declining, it continues to commit significant resources, obligating over $1 billion for TCB-related activities in fiscal years 2011 and 2012. TCB also contributes to meeting goals outlined in USAID and State's Joint Strategic Plan.[16]

Given the changes in the TCB environment since 2003, updating the strategy to reflect those changes could put USAID missions in a better position to select and implement TCB activities. Moreover, an updated strategy could provide USAID missions with important information on changing priorities and lessons learned from evaluations and other assessments, which could also help guide their investments in TCB activities. The outdated nature of some parts of the strategy and the fact that it was released over 10 years ago may also limit its use. Multiple USAID officials we met with in the field were not aware that the strategy existed and did not use it. The number of agencies involved in TCB, and its crosscutting nature, calls for collaboration and coordination to ensure that TCB assistance is meeting U.S. objectives. A USAID official reported that USAID involved relevant agencies in the development of the 2003 TCB strategy to achieve interagency buy-in. However, several other agencies, primarily MCC, have since begun providing TCB assistance. In the absence of an updated strategy, these agencies may be less aware of USAID's TCB priorities and may miss opportunities to leverage resources and ensure that their activities complement USAID's efforts.

USAID Uses Various Methods to Coordinate Trade Capacity Building Activities with Other Agencies

At Headquarters, USAID Participates in Coordinating Bodies and Uses Informal Dialogue to Coordinate TCB Activities

The 2003 strategy calls for USAID to be the primary coordinator for U.S. government TCB efforts, and we found that USAID headquarters staff participate in coordinating bodies, such as interagency working groups, and maintain ongoing discussions with relevant counterparts to coordinate TCB activities. One coordinating body USAID uses is the Trade Policy Staff

Committee (TPSC), a USTR-chaired interagency working group that includes a broad range of stakeholders, meets multiple times a year, and has subcommittees focused on development and TCB. According to a USTR official, the TPSC's subcommittees provide channels for USAID to identify developing country trade capacity needs and opportunities. For example, USAID participates in the TPSC Development and Trade Capacity subcommittee, which focuses on topics such as WTO policy and agreements. In this forum, USAID may discuss needs associated with WTO accession with USTR and other agencies to see if an acceding developing country needs help understanding or meeting requirements. The subcommittee communicates informally and meets on an ad hoc basis, but USAID relies on it as a vehicle to identify ways agencies can leverage TCB resources, according to officials.

The USAID Standards Alliance is an example of project-level coordination. The Alliance involves U.S. government trade and regulatory agencies, as well as the private sector, to address trade barriers. Officially introduced in November 2012, the Standards Alliance is a public-private partnership between USAID and the American National Standards Institute, a private non-profit organization whose membership is made up of businesses, professional societies, trade associations, standards developers, and consumer and labor organizations. The Alliance provides capacity-building assistance to developing countries specifically related to the implementation of the WTO Technical Barriers to Trade Agreement. According to USAID, assistance aims to help developing countries improve the quality and safety of the products they export abroad and increase exports, while reducing costs and bureaucratic hurdles. In addition, Standards Alliance activities are implemented in collaboration with USTR and draw heavily on expertise and technical support from other U.S. agencies including the Department of Commerce/National Institute of Standards and Technology and the Consumer Product Safety Commission. In 2013, USAID worked with the Standards Alliance to conduct workshops in Peru that brought together industry representatives and government officials to discuss U.S. and Peruvian experiences and perspectives related to standardization and regulatory practices. About 130 individuals took part in the event, representing a mix of stakeholders in government, industry, testing and certification bodies, and academia.

USAID also reports using other mechanisms, such as shared management structures and cross-agency agreements, to facilitate TCB coordination. For example, the Administrator of USAID sits on the MCC Board of Directors and contributes to the approval of MCC compacts. According to USAID officials, this shared management structure is intended to ensure stakeholder involvement and provides an opportunity to leverage resources on TCB matters. In addition, USAID is represented on the board of the Overseas Private Investment Corporation (OPIC) and contributes to the approval of OPIC deals, which may have TCB-related components.17 The USAID Office of Development Credit and OPIC also hold quarterly meetings to discuss project plans and other issues of relevance to both units to help ensure relevant skills and expertise are being utilized for TCB and other activities, according to USAID. In addition to shared management structures, a USAID official reported that it has agreements and works with other agencies that play relatively small roles in TCB, such as the Trade and Development Agency and the Departments of Justice and Labor. Involving stakeholders in this way facilitates leveraging TCB resources, according to a USAID official. For example, in Bangladesh, USAID and the Department of Labor are cooperating on implementation of a program to improve labor conditions, promote independent and democratic labor unions, and support labor rights and worker representation. Such activities fall in line with USAID's TCB objective to address labor issues related to trade and to leverage expertise from across the U.S. government.

In addition to using mechanisms that facilitate coordination, officials at USAID, State, and USTR, told us that they discuss TCB matters frequently and on an ad hoc basis, particularly at the staff level. As TCB needs, opportunities, or issues arise, relevant stakeholders communicate informally to coordinate, according to a USTR official. For example, State's Office of Multilateral Trade Affairs monitors trade-related activities and considers how State could help with TCB. The office coordinates with USAID and USTR counterparts and may suggest TCB opportunities related to free trade agreement (FTA) negotiations or WTO obligations in certain countries, according to a State official. A USTR official also told us that USTR shares its annual TCB priorities with USAID and State using an unofficial document that outlines an inventory of possible efforts. This document provides a notional framework that facilitates informal dialogue and stakeholder involvement.

Abroad, USAID Uses Formal Mechanisms and Informal Dialogue with Stakeholders to Coordinate TCB Activities

In countries we visited, including Ethiopia, Tanzania, Vietnam, and Laos, we found that USAID uses certain formal mechanisms, such as working groups, and informal dialogue with stakeholders to coordinate TCB. According to officials we met, in most locations, USAID participates in a formal embassy working group that addresses TCB matters and involves a range of stakeholders, sometimes including the Chief of Mission. Specifically, in countries we visited, we found the following:

- *Ethiopia.* According to officials we met with, USAID coordinates TCB activities primarily through the Economic Growth and Development working group, which meets monthly. This interagency group, one of five created about a year ago under an ambassadorial directive to address the highest-level embassy priorities, covers TCB matters and related topics, such as WTO accession progress and upcoming visits of U.S. government or private sector personnel. Generally, the Chief of Mission and the USAID Mission Director or their deputies report that they attend the meeting, along with representatives from the Foreign Agricultural Service, USAID, and State. Embassy officials told us that this formal channel, along with frequent informal communication among stakeholders, helps ensure a whole-ofgovernment approach to TCB.
- *Tanzania.* According to officials we met with, USAID and its counterparts discuss TCB and development issues at the embassy's biweekly Governance and Prosperity Working Group. The group includes participants from State, USAID, and MCC, and covers ongoing TCB initiatives and development issues. USAID and relevant agencies also may discuss TCB at the embassy's Power Africa working group, a regular meeting that focuses on power and energy sector projects, which may have trade-related effects such as improving competitiveness or capacity.[18] Officials told us that informal communication about TCB matters occurs frequently on an ad hoc basis as well, helping to ensure that resources and expertise across agencies are fully leveraged.
- *Vietnam.* According to officials we met with, the main mechanism through which TCB is coordinated is the interagency commercial task force, which convenes stakeholders from USAID, State, and other relevant agencies weekly. The embassy Deputy Chief of Mission sets the agenda for the task force and participants provide updates on active projects, issues, and policy considerations related to TCB and commercial activities. According to embassy officials, TCB is a key embassy priority and requires a broad range of engagement with the

host government, so coordination is critical. In addition, these officials noted that USAID and its counterparts interact frequently and maintain good working relationships, providing an appropriate environment to enable stakeholders to leverage the range of TCB resources at the embassy.

- *Laos*. According to officials we met with, USAID coordinates its TCB activities in Laos from its regional office in Thailand. USAID does not have a mission in Laos, although it does have a USAID representative (a U.S. Personal Services Contractor) located in the U.S. embassy in Laos who helps to coordinate USAID regional and bilateral projects, including TCB activities. According to a USAID official, TCB efforts in Laos are relatively small and focused, so formal coordination structures are not necessary or practical. Instead, this official explained that the USAID representative regularly liaises with the State Economics Officer, who meets with the Ambassador weekly. Although no official working group has been established, the Economic Officer, Ambassador, and USAID representative meet at least quarterly to discuss TCB assistance. These discussions help to ensure conflicts are avoided and resources are used effectively. Because economic development and TCB projects have been key priorities of the embassy in Laos in recent years, USAID communicates frequently with State counterparts in-country, according to an official. In addition, another official told us that USAID and State worked together to develop the Integrated Country Strategy for Laos, helping to ensure that TCB fit into a common set of interagency goals and priorities.

USAID Has Taken Steps to Use Evaluations in Its Management of TCB Activities

At the Headquarters Level, USAID Has Introduced a Web-based Tool and Taken Other Actions in Response to its 2010 Evaluation

At the headquarters level, USAID officials noted that they have introduced a web-based tool and taken various actions, such as committing to regularly identify best practices, based on the multicountry evaluation completed in 2010. In 2013, USAID launched a web-based tool, called "Project Starter," designed to bring together guidance, templates, examples, and checklists to facilitate monitoring, evaluation, and adaptive learning in TCB activities. From January 1, 2014, through March 31, 2014, the Project Starter website had nearly 4,000 visitors, including a mix of technical, program, and managerial staff from headquarters and the field.

In our 2011 report, we found that USAID had commissioned a limited number of evaluations of TCB programs to assess long-term results, in part because of the resources required and the difficulty of evaluating impact in the area of TCB. We recommended that USAID develop a written plan for using the 2010 multicountry evaluation and conduct further evaluations on an ongoing basis. As a result of our recommendation, USAID committed to conduct every 5 years an analysis of evaluations completed by missions, to identify best practices for trade projects. However, USAID has not incorporated lessons learned identified in the 2010 multicountry evaluation into its TCB strategy.

USAID officials at headquarters also told us that they provide guidance to field staff to facilitate TCB program management, leveraging best practices and lessons learned from evaluations and experience. For example, subject matter experts at headquarters regularly respond to requests for assistance from field staff on designing or evaluating projects. In addition, headquarters staff helped in the design and award of TCB activities in Jordan, Laos, Ghana, Afghanistan, Tanzania, Nigeria, Pakistan, and USAID regional missions in Thailand and West Africa. These activities account for approximately 60 percent of USAID fiscal year 2013 trade funds, according to USAID. In addition, headquarters officials report they provided support for evaluations, results frameworks, and strategy development, to field staff in Morocco, Liberia, West Bank-Gaza, Kenya, and South Africa.

Abroad, USAID Field Staff Have Used Evaluations to Manage Projects at the Country Level

Abroad, USAID field staff have used evaluations and assessments of projects to manage current and future TCB efforts in the countries we visited. During fieldwork, we found that USAID field staff had conducted evaluations and assessments of specific activities and used the information to make changes to ongoing or planned projects as follows:

- *Ethiopia.* USAID conducted a cost-benefit analysis of its support for agricultural value chain projects in 2012, designed to improve productivity and efficiency, among other things. USAID officials told us that based on the analysis, they changed the investment allocation while projects were under way to favor those with better potential for results. In addition, USAID's Ethiopia CDCS calls for elevating the role of evaluations and impact assessments as learning tools throughout the project cycle for continuous updating and promotion of best practices. Officials indicated that the CDCS is the central guiding document for USAID TCB and other activities in-country and that, in accordance with this directive, continuous improvement processes are part of regular operations.
- *Tanzania.* In 2011, USAID's East Africa Trade Hub in Kenya—a regional mission that plays a significant role in managing TCB projects in Tanzania—conducted an assessment of its activities and made changes as a result, according to an official. For example, the assessment recommended that the Trade Hub work with the embassies in the countries it covers, including Tanzania, to develop a shared vision and to facilitate mutually beneficial relationships. According to a USAID official, the Trade Hub responded by taking steps to address this issue. Specifically, the Trade Hub committed to send a person to visit each embassy in the region at least once a year to discuss goals and priorities, and it provided additional country-specific information on its website so stakeholders could see and monitor its activities anytime. The assessment also recommended that the Trade Hub shift to assisting the East Africa Community, a regional economic group that includes Tanzania, and national authorities with the implementation of policies and procedures. As a result, the Trade Hub reallocated some of its TCB resources away from supporting trade-related business development activities to supporting the East Africa Community, its five members, and regional trade associations focused on regional policy implementation, according to a USAID official.
- *Vietnam.* USAID conducted a performance evaluation of STAR, its main TCB activity, in 2011. One of the evaluation's recommendations was that USAID should focus its future efforts on trade facilitation activities, such as improving customs, transportation, and the commercial regulatory environment. According to the evaluation, this would benefit the trading community and help the host government implement and enforce some of the legal and regulatory reforms put in

place over recent years with the support of STAR. A USAID official told us that in response to the recommendation, they designed TCB activities to focus on leveraging relationships with the host government's customs ministry. Specifically, they targeted support toward streamlining customs procedures and regulations with the aim of helping the government and business build on prior reforms. A USAID official also told us that one lesson learned over the years was that involving multiple host government ministries in TCB projects may slow progress. To address this weakness, USAID shifted its approach to focus on a limited number of areas with committed stakeholders while maintaining an ad hoc mechanism for other ministries as needs and opportunities arise.

- *Laos*. Because USAID does not have a presence in Laos, officials told us that they regularly monitor TCB activities in Laos from the regional office in Thailand, working in close coordination with the USAID representative in Laos and embassy staff. They also indicated that early TCB work in Laos focused on establishing a basic legal framework to meet WTO requirements, but as a result of monitoring and evaluating progress, USAID shifted the focus of assistance to facilitating implementation of the laws and regulations put in place. A USAID official also told us that this year they are updating a Lao Business and Commercial Law and Institutional Reform assessment that will provide a baseline for the new TCB assistance for Laos.

CONCLUSION

The U.S. government continues to demonstrate a commitment to providing TCB for developing countries, and over the years multiple U.S. agencies have provided this assistance across numerous types of trade and development programs. Given the diffused nature of TCB assistance, Congress has expressed concern about which agency is ultimately accountable for TCB activities. While no single agency is responsible for this type of assistance, USAID has a 2003 TCB strategy that defines overall TCB priorities and discusses coordination with other U.S. agencies. In addition, in fiscal year 2012, USAID provided about $418 million for TCB, the most funding of any U.S. government agency. Therefore, it is important that USAID's strategy reflect the current TCB environment. USAID officials asserted that the priorities in the strategy are still relevant, but we observed that neither USAID nor other agency officials we met with in the field used, or in some cases even knew about, the strategy. Moreover, we found that the strategy may not be as useful as it could be because it is outdated in several areas. For example, the coordination section of the strategy does not include all agencies now providing TCB assistance, the trade initiatives discussed in the strategy are no longer current, and the categories of TCB activities identified in the strategy have changed. Updating the strategy to reflect the current TCB environment would provide USAID an opportunity to examine its TCB priorities in light of changes to the environment and ensure that the priorities are indeed still relevant. A strategy update would also raise awareness of the agency's TCB priorities in relevant missions and offices. In the absence of a government-wide TCB strategy, an effort to update the USAID TCB strategy could also bring together other agencies involved in providing TCB assistance, helping to ensure interagency buy-in on current TCB priorities and goals.

Recommendation for Executive Action

To help ensure that USAID's 2003 TCB strategy is as useful as it could be for informing TCB activities, we recommend that the Administrator of USAID update the strategy to reflect the current TCB environment.

Agency Comments and Our Evaluation

We requested comments on a draft of this report from the Administrator of USAID, the Secretary of State, the Chief Executive Officer of the Millennium Challenge Corporation, and the U.S. Trade Representative.

On July 15, 2014, USAID indicated via e-mail that it agreed with the recommendation and intended to explore options for providing additional guidance to operating units. USAID further indicated that the additional guidance might take the form of drafting a new TCB strategy, updating or amending the old strategy, issuing a separate policy paper, contributing to a broader U.S. government-wide strategy, or some other type of guidance. In its written comments, MCC stated that it was in the process of updating the MCC data in the U.S. government TCB database. We did not receive comments from State or USTR.

Sincerely yours,

Kimberly Gianopoulos
Acting Director,
International Affairs and Trade

APPENDIX I: USAID AND STATE TRADE CAPACITY BUILDING FUNDING DATA, FISCAL YEARS 2011 THROUGH 2012

In fiscal years 2011 through 2012, the U.S. Agency for International Development (USAID) and the Department of State (State) together obligated a total of approximately $1.36 billion for trade capacity building (TCB) related activities. Of that amount, USAID obligated approximately $1.1 billion with funds from seven different accounts. State obligated the approximately $262 million remaining, with funds from seven funding accounts. (See table 1 below.) USAID officials noted that there is no dedicated funding account or directive for TCB activities. USAID officials also noted that the majority of the TCB assistance reported in the database are obligations for development projects that had trade-related effects—and were therefore counted as TCB—but were conducted to fulfill other development objectives.

Table 1. USAID and State Obligations for Trade Capacity Building Related Activities by Funding Account, Fiscal Years 2011 through 2012

Funding agency and account	2011	2012
U.S. Agency for International Development		
Assistance for Eastern Europe and the Baltic States	$350,000	$1,900,000
Assistance for Europe, Eurasia, and Central Asia	$60,269,640	$29,243,598
Assistance for the Independent States of the Former Soviet Union	$5,371,030	$5,495,820
Development Assistance	$292,365,424	$173,071,344
Development Credit Authority, United States	$604,608	-
Economic Support Fund	$327,630,138	$206,397,931
Sub-Saharan Africa, Development Assistance	-	$1,900,000

Table 1. (Continued)

Funding agency and account	2011	2012
Total (U.S. Agency for International Development)	$686,590,840	$418,008,693
Department of State		
Democracy Fund, Department of State	$448,000	-
Educational and Cultural Exchange Programs, Department of State	$43,929,157	$56,652,219
Global Health and Child Survival	-	$690,000
International Organizations and Programs	$20,059,207	$18,847,889
International Narcotics Control and Law Enforcement[a]	$3,904,091	$5,219,385
Iraq Relief and Reconstruction Fund, Executive Office of the President[a]	$61,902	-
Nonproliferation, Anti-Terrorism, Demining and Related Programs[a]	$50,999,493	$61,545,538
Total (Department of State)	$119,401,850	$142,955,031
Total (Both USAID and State)	$805,992,690	$560,963,724

Source: USAID. | GAO-14-602.

Legend: USAID = U.S. Agency for International Development, State = Department of State.

[a] According to USAID, the International Narcotics Control and Law Enforcement, Department of State; Iraq Relief and Reconstruction Fund, Executive Office of the President; and Nonproliferation, Anti-Terrorism, Demining and Related Programs, Department of State are funding accounts under the Executive Office of the President that are assigned to the Department of State, as State largely manages the funds in these accounts and is responsible for reporting on them.

Appendix II: Objectives, Scope, and Methodology

Our objectives were to (1) determine the extent to which the U.S. Agency for International Development's (USAID) 2003 strategy guides USAID's trade capacity building (TCB) activities; (2) describe methods USAID uses to coordinate TCB efforts with other U.S. government agencies at home and abroad; and (3) describe how, if at all, USAID has used TCB evaluations in its program and project management. For fiscal years 2011 and 2012, we also identified the appropriations accounts from which USAID and State allocated funds for TCB-related activities and the obligations from these accounts for such activities (see app. I).

To address these objectives, we built upon information collected for our 2005 and 2011 reports on TCB and analyzed data from the U.S. government TCB database. Data from the TCB database were previously deemed reliable for our 2005 and 2011 reports on TCB. We identified limitations to the TCB database in our 2011 report on TCB, including that the database did not adequately explain significant factors driving changes in the composition of TCB funding over time. For this 2014 report on TCB, we assessed data from fiscal years 2008 through 2012 and determined that the data were sufficiently reliable to identify TCB funding by agency, country, and category.[1] Furthermore, in assessing the data, we interviewed key USAID officials and the contractor responsible for administering the database, and reviewed supporting documentation.

We primarily focused on TCB activities that USAID conducted because USAID provided the most funding of all U.S. agencies for TCB activities in 2012. However, we also sought the views of three other entities in our review regarding coordination with USAID on TCB activities: (1) the Department of State (State) because it is committed to supporting the negotiation and implementation of trade agreements and thereby helps countries advance trade initiatives; (2) the Millennium Challenge Corporation (MCC) because it conducts TCB-related activities that support its broader strategic and agency mission goals, although it does not have a specific TCB mission; and (3) the Office of the U.S. Trade Representative (USTR) because of its role in leading trade efforts. In conducting our work, we analyzed strategic, budget, and programmatic documents describing these agencies' TCB-related funding and activities. We also reviewed the 2010 TCB evaluation, along with evaluations and assessments of TCB projects in the countries we visited. We conducted fieldwork in Vietnam, Laos, Thailand, Ethiopia, Tanzania, and Kenya. We selected these countries because they (1) had a cross-section of projects that would allow us to compare and contrast different types of activities, (2) are at different stages of economic development, (3) are in diverse geographic regions, or (4) had signed an MCC compact and received MCC-related TCB assistance. In each country, we analyzed agencies' strategy, coordination, and program management efforts. We also interviewed agency officials, host government officials, and contractors implementing TCB activities in the field, and visited TCB project sites. Our findings from these countries are not generalizable to the universe of all USAID TCB activities.

To determine the extent to which USAID's 2003 strategy guides USAID's TCB activities, we reviewed the strategy and relevant documents and interviewed USAID officials in Washington, D.C.; Ethiopia; Kenya; Laos;

Tanzania; Thailand; and Vietnam about what they use to guide TCB activities in their countries. We also interviewed these officials about the agencies' TCB priorities and the relevance of the strategy to the current environment. We reviewed guidance on strategic planning from several sources, including USAID's internal policies, the Government Performance and Results Act Modernization Act of 2010, and prior GAO work on strategic planning, for criteria on updating strategies. We did not review USAID's 2003 TCB strategy using the full set of six characteristics of a national strategy that we identified in prior work; we determined that many of the characteristics may not apply to it because it is only an agency document and not a national strategy. However, in reviewing the strategy we did examine the extent to which it reflected the current TCB environment, because the strategy was developed over 10 years ago. TCB environment refers to the context—including all conditions, entities, events, and surrounding factors—in which agencies providing TCB assistance are operating.

To describe methods USAID uses to coordinate TCB efforts with other U.S. government agencies at home and abroad, we interviewed officials from USAID, State, USTR, and MCC, and analyzed relevant documents. During our fieldwork, we also spoke with officials from other agencies, such as the U.S. Department of Agriculture and the Department of Commerce, which in some cases play a role in TCB activities. We used GAO's prior work on collaboration, which reports on collaboration mechanisms and key practices for consideration, to develop our interview questions for USAID and other agency officials, and to help identify actions USAID has taken.[2] However, we did not formally assess USAID's TCB coordination with other agencies.

To describe how, if at all, USAID has used TCB evaluations in its program and project management, we interviewed officials from USAID and analyzed relevant documents. During our fieldwork, we reviewed evaluations and assessments of projects in the countries we visited. We did not assess the challenges or effectiveness of TCB measurement and evaluation processes in place because we addressed these issues in our 2011 report. [3]

We conducted this performance audit from October 2013 to August 2014 in accordance with generally accepted government auditing standards. Those standards require that we plan and perform the audit to obtain sufficient, appropriate evidence to provide a reasonable basis for our findings and conclusions based on our audit objectives. We believe that the evidence obtained provides a reasonable basis for our findings and conclusions based on our audit objectives.

APPENDIX III: U.S. GOVERNMENT TRADE CAPACITY BUILDING DATABASE AND DEFINITIONAL CATEGORIES

TCB Database

As we previously noted in 2011, the U.S. Agency for International Development (USAID) collects data to identify and quantify the U.S. government's trade capacity building (TCB) activities in developing countries through an annual survey of agencies on behalf of the Office of the U.S. Trade Representative (USTR), and oversees a contractor that collects and maintains the survey results in the U.S. government's publicly available online TCB database.[1] The data gathered from this survey are used to inform and respond to inquiries from Congress, the executive branch, the general public, and multilateral organizations such as the World Trade Organization (WTO). USTR officials use the database regularly and, according to these officials, it is a useful tool for identifying U.S. agencies' TCB activities and funding in a particular country or region, as well as the full extent of assistance the U.S. government provides in that area. In addition to administering this survey, USAID is also tasked with reviewing completed survey forms, and checking for accuracy and consistency in the reporting of funding and their allocation into TCB categories. A variety of U.S. agencies have a role in providing TCB assistance, including the Departments of State, the Army, Labor, the Treasury, and Commerce; the Millennium Challenge Corporation (MCC); and USAID.

TCB Category Definitions

USAID's survey asks agencies to place their TCB assistance into a range of categories and estimate funding obligated for each category. The U.S. government TCB database defines the categories as follows:

- WTO Accession and Compliance: Support for countries to benefit from membership in the WTO, or to understand fully the benefits of membership. Also assistance to help countries in the WTO accession process meet the requirements of accession. In addition, it includes assistance to meet the obligations of the specific WTO agreements, except for Agreements on Sanitary and Phyto-sanitary Measures

(SPS), Technical Barriers to Trade (TBT), Intellectual Property Rights (IPR), and Trade-related Procurement. Those four agreements benefit from TCB in their own categories.

- Sanitary and Phyto-Sanitary Measures: Support for countries to meet SPS standards for trade and to comply with the WTO Agreement on SPS.
- Technical Barriers to Trade: Support for countries to reduce technical barriers to trade and to comply with the WTO Agreement on TBT.
- Intellectual Property Rights: Support for countries to observe international standards on intellectual property rights protection and to comply with the WTO Agreement on IPR.
- Trade-related Procurement: Support for increased trade related to government procurement and to comply with the WTO Agreement on Government Procurement.
- Trade Facilitation: Generally defined as assistance in lowering the costs of engaging in, or eliminating obstacles to international trade flows. Trade facilitation (for 2011) is a sum of the following four subcategories:
  - Customs Operations: Includes assistance to help countries modernize and improve their customs offices.
  - Trade Promotion: Includes assistance to increase market opportunities for developing country and transition economy producers.
  - Enterprise Development: Includes support to improve the associations and networks in the business sector, as well as to enhance the skills of business people engaged in trade. Also includes assistance to help countries acquire and use information technology to promote trade by creating business networks and disseminating market information.
  - FTAs and Trade Integration: Includes assistance to an FTA, an regional trade agreement, or to an individual country that increases the ability of the RTA to facilitate trade. It can also include assistance to a potential member of an RTA that improves the analytical capacity of the country's government with respect to RTA issues. (Note: It does not include TCB assistance in a specific area that is being provided to countries through an RTA. For example, technical assistance to help RTA member countries comply with SPS standards was reported as Trade-Related

Agricultural Development or the WTO Agreement on SPS Measures.)

- Trade-related Labor: Assistance to support the enforcement of labor standards and worker rights, development of trade unions and dispute resolution mechanisms, strategies for workforce development and worker training, and the elimination of child labor.
- Financial Sector: Support for financial sector work, monetary and fiscal policy, exchange rates, commodity markets, and capital markets.
- Trade-related Infrastructure: Assistance to establish trade-related telecoms, transport, ports, airports, power, water, and industrial zones.
- Environmental Sector Trade and Standards: Assistance to establish environmental standards or to promote environmental technology.
- Competition Policy, Business Environment, and Governance: Support for the design and implementation of antitrust laws, as well as of laws and regulations related to investment and investor protections. Includes support for legal and institutional reform to improve governance and make policies more transparent, and assistance to help the different agencies of a host country government function more effectively in the trade policy arena.
- Trade-related Agriculture: Support for trade-related aspects of the agriculture and agribusiness sectors. (Note: Support that is specifically intended to help countries participate in the WTO Agreements on Agriculture or SPS Measures is not included in this category.)
- Trade-related Services: Includes support to help developing countries and transition economies increase their flows of trade in services. Services Trade Development is a sum of two subcategories:
    - Trade-related Services (excluding tourism): Assistance to help countries develop trade in services in all sectors other than tourism, including financial services, energy, transportation, and education.
    - Trade-related Tourism: Assistance to help countries expand their international tourism sectors, including eco-tourism.
- Other Trade Capacity Building: A small number of TCB activities did not fit in any of the above categories, including some activities of a crosscutting nature. These were categorized as “Other Trade Capacity Building.”

End Notes

[1] GAO, Foreign Assistance: The United States Provides Wide-ranging Trade Capacity Building Assistance, but Better Reporting and Evaluation Are Needed, GAO-11-727 (Washington, D.C.: July 29, 2011). As we previously reported in GAO-11-727, USAID collects data to identify and quantify the U.S. government's TCB activities in developing countries through an annual survey of agencies on behalf of the Office of the U.S. Trade Representative (USTR), and oversees a contractor that collects and maintains the survey results in the U.S. government's publicly available online TCB database, accessed May 27, 2014, http://tcb.eads.usaidallnet.gov. USAID's survey asks agencies to place their TCB assistance into a range of categories and estimate funding obligated for each category.

[2] USAID, USAID Strategy: Building Trade Capacity in the Developing World, PD-ABX-241 (Washington, D.C.: March 2003).

[3] GAO, Foreign Assistance: U.S. Trade Capacity Building Extensive, but Its Effectiveness Has Yet to Be Evaluated, GAO-05-150 (Washington, D.C.: Feb. 11, 2005), GAO-11-727, and the U.S. government TCB database, accessed May 28, 2014, http://tcb.eads.usaidallnet.gov/.

[4] In order to present the most current data, GAO accessed the USAID TCB database on August 5, 2014. As of that date, the latest data available was from fiscal year 2012.

[5] According to USAID, a majority of the agency's obligations reported in the U.S. government TCB database reflect activities that are implemented to achieve development objectives other than TCB. USAID's Trade and Investment program area funds, when obligated, are related to TCB and are informed by USAID's TCB strategy, according to USAID.

[6] According to USAID's 2003 TCB strategy, participation in trade negotiations includes helping government decision makers to develop the skills to participate fully in international trade negotiations, analyze their effect, and build domestic support for negotiating positions and the international commitments that result. Implementation of trade agreements includes building both human and institutional capacities that are required to implement commitments made in the course of multilateral, regional, and bilateral trade negotiations. Helping developing countries take advantage of the opportunities created by trade includes support for countries' efforts to strengthen economic policies; remove trade barriers; build well-functioning economic, political, and legal institutions; improve regulatory policies that affect the way firms compete; and improve private sector operating practices and strategies.

[7] The Doha Development Agenda was the result of World Trade Organization (WTO) negotiations begun in 2001 in Doha, Qatar. The agenda recognized that (1) continued multilateral trade liberalization is necessary to accelerate growth and poverty reduction in developing countries and (2) specific steps must be taken to help developing countries take advantage of the opportunities created by trade liberalization.

[8] According to its website, Feed the Future is the U.S. government's global hunger and food security initiative, targeted to help reduce the effects of extreme poverty, undernutrition, and hunger. To achieve this goal, Feed the Future agencies work with partner countries to develop their agriculture sectors and break the cycle of poverty and hunger. Led by USAID, Feed the Future draws on the agricultural, trade, investment, development and policy resources and expertise of 10 U.S. agencies. Accessed May 29, 2014, http://www.feedthefuture.gov/.

[9] The Staples Value Chain Development project is part of USAID's Feed the Future initiative in Tanzania and aligns with the Feed the Future goal to harmonize regional hunger- and poverty-fighting efforts in countries with chronic food insecurity and insufficient production of staple crops.

[10] The TCB environment refers to the context—including all conditions, entities, events, and surrounding factors—in which agencies providing TCB assistance are operating.

[11] Sec. 2 of Pub. L. No. 111-352, 124 Stat. 3866 at 3867. The Government Performance and Results Act Modernization Act of 2010 amends the Government Performance and Results Act of 1993, Pub. L. No. 103-62, 107 Stat 285 (1993).

[12] In prior work, we identified six desirable characteristics for strategies. See GAO-04-408T, Combating Terrorism: Evaluation of Selected Characteristics in National Strategies Related to Terrorism (Washington, D.C.: Feb. 3, 2004). To develop the characteristics, we reviewed several sources of information, including statutory requirements pertaining to national strategies, the Government Performance and Results Act of 1993, and general literature on strategic planning and performance. In addition, among other things, we studied past reports and testimonies for findings and recommendations pertaining to the desirable elements of a national strategy.

[13] Management Systems International, "From Aid to Trade: Delivering Results: A Cross-Country Evaluation of USAID Trade Capacity Building" (Washington, D.C.: Nov. 24, 2010).

[14] In August 2013, in responding to GAO's recommendations in GAO-11-727, USAID reported that it was updating its TCB strategy in response to the recommendation in the 2010 evaluation. As of June 2014, there were no updates to the strategy.

[15] In a report on strategic planning, we found that for the planning to be effective, three practices are critical. Organizations must (1) involve their stakeholders, (2) assess their internal and external environments, and (3) align their activities, core processes, and resources to support mission-related outcomes. See Agencies' Strategic Plans Under GPRA: Key Questions to Facilitate Congressional Review, GAO/GGD-10.1.16 (Washington, D.C.: May 1997).

[16] In USAID and State's fiscal years 2014-2017 Joint Strategic Plan, TCB activities are being used to help achieve both objectives under the strategic goal of strengthening America's economic reach and positive economic impact. The objectives are (1) to expand access to future markets, investments, and trade; and (2) to promote inclusive economic growth, reduce extreme poverty, and improve food security.

[17] OPIC is a U.S. government development finance institution that provides investors with financing, guarantees, and political risk insurance, among other things. In pursuit of its mission objectives, OPIC at times supports TCB-related activities. For example, in 2012, OPIC supported a project designed to provide loans to agricultural cooperatives in 42 countries for the production and export of commodities such as bananas, cocoa, and coffee.

[18] Announced in June 2013 by the President of the United States, Power Africa is an initiative to double access to power in sub-Saharan Africa. Initial partner countries include Ethiopia, Ghana, Kenya, Liberia, Nigeria, and Tanzania.

End Notes for Appendix II

[1] In 2011, we found that the U.S. government TCB database did not adequately explain significant factors driving changes in the composition of TCB funding over time or factors that underlie the increase in annual funding from $1.35 billion in 2005 to $1.69 billion in 2010. We recommended that USAID publicly report identified limitations and key distinctions in the categories of TCB assistance in the database. See GAO-11-727. In response to the recommendation, USAID streamlined and clarified the definitions of TCB

categories to facilitate reporting and improve transparency. This change was reflected in the "technical notes" section of the TCB database. In addition, USAID noted on the TCB database website that, for many TCB activities in the database, the funding level does not match up with the fiscal year or years in which the activity is in operation or being funded.

[2] GAO, Managing for Results: Key Considerations for Implementing Interagency Collaborative Mechanisms, GAO-12-1022 (Washington, D.C.: Sept. 27, 2012); and GAO, Results-Oriented Government: Practices That Can Help Enhance and Sustain Collaboration among Federal Agencies, GAO-06-15 (Washington, D.C.: Oct. 21, 2005).

[3] GAO-11-727.

End Note for Appendix III

[1] See GAO-11-727, p. 4-5.

In: Trade Capacity Building
Editor: Richard T. Royce

ISBN: 978-1-63463-733-6

Chapter 3

USAID STRATEGY: BUILDING TRADE CAPACITY IN THE DEVELOPING WORLD*

U.S. Agency for International Development

EXECUTIVE SUMMARY

The Relationship Between Trade and Development

Integration into the global economy can be a powerful force for economic growth and poverty reduction. In its recent *National Security Strategy,* the Bush administration established the goal of igniting a new era of global economic growth through free markets and free trade.

Trade and investment are the principal mechanisms through which global market forces—competition, human resource development, technology transfer, and technological innovation—generate growth in developing and developed countries. During the 1990s, developing countries that successfully integrated into the global economy enjoyed per capita income increases averaging 5 percent annually. However, countries that limited their participation in the global economy saw their economies decline.

Developing countries' overall share of global trade is increasing, and the flow of foreign direct investment to poor countries has grown rapidly. But this growth is concentrated in a few countries, and many of the poorest developing

---

* This is an edited, reformatted and augmented version of USAID document, PD-ABX-241, issued March 2003.

countries remain on the sidelines. Not surprisingly, development issues have become increasingly prominent in international trade negotiations. The Doha Development Agenda recognizes that continued multilateral trade liberalization is necessary to accelerate growth and reduce poverty in developing countries and that World Trade Organization (WTO) member countries must help developing countries build their capacity to take advantage of trade liberalization. USAID trade capacity building (TCB) assistance programs—$423 million in FY2001 and $476 million in FY2002—are already helping developing countries to integrate themselves into the global economy.

THE CONCEPTUAL FRAMEWORK: PARTICIPATION, IMPLEMENTATION, AND ECONOMIC RESPONSIVENESS

While ongoing programs address a variety of TCB needs, a conceptual framework is needed to focus USAID's efforts and guide the selection of new activities. The agency's goal is to increase the number of developing and transition countries that are harnessing global economic forces to accelerate growth and increase incomes. To this end, USAID's trade capacity building projects will support the following:

- *Participation in trade negotiations.* Government decisionmakers, in consultation with the private sector and civil society, need the skills to participate fully in international trade negotiations, analyze their effect, and build domestic support for negotiating positions and the international commitments that result.
- *Implementation of trade agreements.* Both human and institutional capacity are required to implement commitments made in the course of multilateral, regional, and bilateral trade negotiations.
- *Economic responsiveness to opportunities for trade.* To promote economic growth, reduce poverty, and sustain support for trade liberalization, developing countries must be able to take advantage of the opportunities created by trade. To do so, developing countries need support for their efforts to strengthen economic policies; remove trade barriers; build well-functioning economic, political, and legal institutions; improve regulatory policies that affect the way firms compete; and improve private sector operating practices and strategies.

USAID's Strategy

USAID will enhance ongoing TCB programs with new initiatives to support developing countries' *participation* in international trade negotiations. USAID will increase support for WTO accessions, help countries develop trade analysis expertise, and enhance the information resources available to trade analysts in partner countries. To support trade agreement *implementation,* USAID will introduce new programs to promote sound systems of commercial law and improved customs management. The agency will also help developing countries establish open and competitive markets in services sectors that are critical to trade. To strengthen *economic responsiveness* to opportunities for trade, USAID will continue to implement a wide range of trade-related economic growth projects that improve economic policies and institutions, transfer technology, reduce dependence on exports of unprocessed tropical agricultural commodities, and assist local private sectors to meet product standards in international markets and take advantage of preferential market access programs.

> USAID's strategy for trade capacity building recognizes that activities are likely to have the greatest impact when they are implemented in reform-minded developing countries.

Specific considerations that will influence the agency's approach to TCB include support for multilateral, regional, and bilateral trade negotiations, particularly bilateral Free Trade Area negotiations with the United States; the trade aspects of labor, gender, and environmental issues; availability of funding; and coordination with U.S. Government agencies and other donors. USAID will work closely with other U.S. Government agencies and through the interagency process to coordinate TCB assistance.

USAID's strategy for trade capacity building recognizes that activities are likely to have the greatest impact when they are implemented in reform-minded developing countries—those that already have made progress in establishing a sound investment climate and in liberalizing financial and other service sectors that support competitive exports.

Next Steps

In parallel with the new activities described above, USAID will continue to build its own capacity to deliver more—and more effective—TCB assistance. Efforts are already underway to build trade into the agency's planning and programs by enhancing staff trade knowledge and skills, requiring country strategies to consider trade and investment, developing best-practice trade and investment tools, and communicating capacity building needs identified in negotiations. USAID will continue to rely on expertise provided by private sector contractors and nongovernmental organizations in implementing the bulk of its TCB projects. The agency will work with country missions to harness the unique capabilities of other U.S. Government agencies where appropriate.

USAID expects the results of this strategy to include more active and better informed participation by developing countries in a range of international trade negotiations and related activities. Results should also include tangible improvements in the effectiveness of developing countries' commercial laws and institutions, and, over time, improvements in the quantity and quality of individual developing country's exports, imports, and foreign investment.

TRADE AND DEVELOPMENT

Developing countries' share of global trade is increasing, and the flow of foreign direct investment (FDI) to poor countries has grown rapidly in recent decades. During the 1990s, developing countries that successfully integrated into the global economy enjoyed per capita income increases on an average of 5 percent annually. Conversely, those countries that protected their domestic markets with tariff barriers and other measures that limited their participation in the global economy saw their economics decline.[1]

At the March 2002 International Financing for Development Conference in Monterrey, Mexico, leaders of developed and developing countries agreed that trade and investment are critical sources of development finance—far outweighing foreign assistance in the broader context of international capital flows. President George W. Bush pointed out that developing countries receive $50 billion a year in aid, while foreign investment inflows total almost $200 billion and annual earnings from exports exceed $2.4 trillion. The president also noted that, in 2001, trade opportunities created by the African Growth and Opportunity Act (AGOA) alone boosted African exports to the United States by more than 1,000 percent, generated nearly $1 billion in investment, and created thousands of jobs.

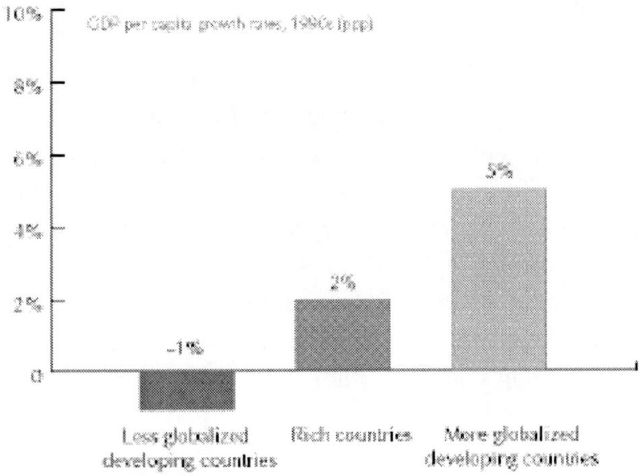

Source: David Dollar and Aart Kraay, "Trade, Growth, and Poverty," 2001. <www.worldbank.org/research/growth/pdfiles/Trade5.pdf>

Figure 1. Globalization and Growth in the 1990s.

It is clear that integration into the global economy can be a powerful force for economic growth and poverty reduction. Trade and investment are the principal mechanisms through which global market forces—competition, human resource development, technology transfer, and technological innovation—generate growth in developing and developed countries. Trade expansion is particularly critical for many of the smallest and poorest developing and transition economies, where local demand is too weak to support rapid expansion of production, employment, and incomes. Integration into the global economy can also enhance economic and social stability, a factor in conflict prevention. Participation in the rules-based trading system reinforces good governance and strengthens legal and institutional reforms, creating a more predictable and conducive environment for mobilizing private finance and generating economic growth. For these and other reasons, fostering developing countries' participation in international trade is a core element of the Bush administration's recent *National Security Strategy of the United States of America.*[2]

While the potential benefits are clear, developing countries' capacities to take advantage of opportunities for trade and investment vary considerably. As a whole, developing countries now supply about one-third of world exports, but China, the Asian newly industrializing economies, and a few oil-producing states account for the lion's share of this total. The 49 least developed countries (LDCs) account for just 2 percent of developing country exports and 0.5 percent of global exports.[3] Similarly, FDI to developing countries has grown dramatically—from $2 billion in 1970 to $240 billion in 2000 (in nominal terms)—but the bulk goes to China and a few other large emerging markets. LDCs receive only a small fraction of the total.[4]

It should be no surprise, then, that development issues have become increasingly prominent in international trade negotiations. In November 2001, members of the WTO launched a new round of negotiations in Doha, Qatar. The negotiating agenda adopted in Qatar has been labeled the "Doha Development Agenda" because WTO members recognized that: 1) continued multilateral trade liberalization is necessary to accelerate growth and poverty reduction in developing countries, and 2) specific steps must be taken to help developing countries take advantage of the opportunities created by trade liberalization. This agenda calls for renewed efforts by donors to help developing country members of the WTO participate more effectively in trade negotiations, comply with and implement existing trade agreements, and improve their economies' competitiveness in the global economy.

USAID is committed to actively supporting the Doha Development Agenda and other trade liberalization initiatives. The agency will continue to step up its support for a broad range of projects that respond to developing countries' TCB needs, as described in Appendix 1 and *United States Government Initiatives to Build Trade Related Capacity in Developing and Transition Countries.*[5] This will include projects that help developing countries participate in international trade negotiations and effectively implement the resulting agreements. It will also address the broad range of reforms and human, institutional, and physical capacity building that will allow these countries' economies to effectively respond to the opportunities created by international trade and investment. A country's effective trading capacity has many dimensions that overlap with the broad needs of economic development (see Appendix 2). USAID will seek to take full advantage of the opportunities that trade capacity building offers to complement and enhance USAID's broader development assistance strategies.

Recognizing that increased ability to trade in a global marketplace is highly correlated with improvements in the local investment climate, and that trade and investment are complementary engines of economic growth, USAID programs under this strategy will focus on TCB assistance rather than on promoting investment per se. A successful strategy for TCB assistance will directly improve developing countries' investment climates.

Trade Capacity Building and The National Security Strategy of the United States of America

The September 2002 *National Security Strategy of the United States* identifies eight goals. One of them is to ignite a new era of global economic growth through free markets and free trade. Another is to "expand the circle of development." These goals are closely linked—the strategy emphasizes that trade and investment are powerful engines of economic growth. USAID's strategy for trade capacity building lies at the intersection of these two goals and reinforces both. It will encourage developing country support for open markets. It will also enhance their capacity to reap the benefits of a rules-based global trading system, thereby accelerating their development progress.

USAID will ensure that its response to partner-country requests for assistance in trade capacity building complies with existing legislative measures intended to protect U.S. trade, investment, and employment.[6] This guidance helps ensure that TCB assistance does not conflict with or undermine USAID's interests in promoting U.S. trade, investment, and employment. Some of this guidance has been in place for a long time and may or may not reflect the current views of Congress. To determine whether changes or new interpretations are warranted, agency staff will review such guidance in view of current U.S. commitments to expanded TCB assistance.

New Opportunities Created by International Negotiations

Over the next few years, trade negotiations will provide great opportunities to generate economic growth in developing countries. Trade capacity building is a fundamental feature of international cooperation in support of these negotiations. Led by the United States, trade ministers of the industrialized countries made an unprecedented commitment at the WTO's Fourth Ministerial Conference in Doha to assist developing countries to benefit from the rules-based trading system. Commitments to capacity building are also contained in other trade forums, such as the Free Trade Area of the Americas (FTAA), Asia Pacific Economic Cooperation (APEC), and negotiations on bilateral free trade area agreements between the United States and a number of developing countries. Because development agencies are expected to supply the required TCB, they have a mandate and a new base of support for promoting economic growth in the developing world.

Over the next few years, a variety of multilateral trade negotiations are likely to yield agreements that create dramatic new opportunities for develop ing countries. Reductions in trade barriers—both in developing countries' export markets and in their internal markets—will improve economic and commercial efficiency and spur economic growth.

Another core objective of those negotiations is to ensure transparency and predictability in economic governance, reinforcing economic reforms that are critical for successful development. For this reason, the concessions a country makes in trade negotiations frequently may have as favorable an impact on its economic growth as the concessions it receives from other countries. The Doha negotiations, for example, offer promise in all these areas. Doha agricultural negotiations are expected to reduce subsidies, tariffs, and nontariff barriers to exports of agricultural commodities that are especially important to developing country economies. Similarly, Doha negotiations on trade in services will encourage countries to increase competition in sectors such as energy, transportation, and telecommunications, where expensive and unreliable supply currently inhibits domestic producers' ability to supply goods and services that meet international standards at competitive prices. Because successful trade negotiations will generally accelerate reforms that can increase economic growth, TCB includes activities that support specific negotiations and build trade capacity generally. The extent and speed with which developing countries take advantage of these opportunities will depend on their own political leadership, supported by TCB assistance from abroad.

Trade Agreements and USAID's Democracy and Governance Objectives

Many WTO and other international trade agreements can act as an international anchor for critical national reforms designed to combat corruption and promote democracy and good governance. Binding commitments to transparency, due process, and public accountability are at the core of these agreements. Many of those agreements—such as those relating to customs, government procurement, and the application of sanitary and phytosanitary (SPS) measures—include procedural requirements that limit discretionary actions by public authorities. Predictable implementation of these procedures can be particularly helpful in strengthening anticorruption efforts.

USAID Trade Capacity Building Efforts

USAID assistance programs are already helping developing countries build the capacity to integrate themselves into the global economy. The programs address a range of issues, including the need for market-friendly tax regimes, sound property rights and commercial law, more diverse and market-responsive agricultural products, reformed financial sectors, and strong business skills (see Appendix 2). Some ongoing projects focus on the trade negotiating process, including support for WTO awareness, accession, and implementation of trade agreements. Others address countries' capaci ties to respond to trade and investment opportunities. A number of programs are explicitly designed to complement U.S. regional trade initiatives, such as the AGOA and FTAA.

The total value of USAID's funding for trade capacity building is increasing—it reached $423 million in FY2001 and $476 million in FY2002. The geographic distribution of these funds reflects the multiple objectives of the U.S. foreign assistance program. Recipients of the largest amount of funds are countries of Eastern Europe and the former Soviet Union, followed by Egypt and Jordan.

TCB funds for LDCs are significant but relatively small—$42.4 million in FY2001, 10 percent of the total. The diversity of fund recipients means that the agency's TCB strategy must be adaptable to different situations and must set clear geographic and programmatic priorities for the application of new activities and funds.

Agriculture, Rural Poverty, and International Trade

Because the world's poorest and most vulnerable populations depend on the health of the rural economy, agricultural development and diversification are critical elements of USAID's economic growth and poverty reduction strategies. Projects that help developing countries participate in agricultural trade negotiations, implement related agreements, and take advantage of opportunities to tap into global food and agricultural commercial networks make important contributions to these efforts. Such projects can spur economic growth and raise incomes by, for example, fostering access to new technologies and providing information and assistance needed to meet regulatory requirements in key markets.

CONCEPTUAL FRAMEWORK

USAID's goal for TCB is to increase the number of developing and transition countries that are harnessing global economic forces to accelerate growth and increase incomes. In pursuit of that goal, TCB activities will help countries meet three strategic requirements for benefiting from the global trading system: *participation, implementation,* and *economic responsiveness.*

Participation in Trade Negotiations

Government decisionmakers, in consultation with the private sector and civil society, need to understand the substance and modalities of international negotiations, analyze the effect of negotiations on national interests, and build domestic consensus for negotiating positions that reflect those interests. TCB activities include

- support for a country's efforts to accede to the WTO and harmonize domestic policies, laws, and regulations with WTO requirements.
- technical support to public and private organizations that provide trade negotiators with analysis of economic impacts and opportunities resulting from trade policy scenarios.
- training in the procedures and modalities for participation in international trade negotiations.

Implementation of Trade Agreements

A country requires both institutional and human capacity to implement commitments made in the course of trade negotiations, acceding to the WTO, or joining a regional trade agreement. Illustrative trade capacity building activities could include

- assistance in implementing WTO requirements for customs valuation, import licensing, and/or rules of origin
- support for a country's efforts to satisfy licensing requirements of AGOA and other preferential trade programs

Economic Responsiveness to Trade Opportunities

Workers, firms, and economies as a whole must be able to respond quickly and efficiently to international market signals to take advantage of trade opportunities and reap the benefits of the international trading system. This means they must be competitive and productive. In USAID's view, competitiveness is essentially a matter of productivity. Competitiveness and productivity are determined by three factors. One factor is the macroenvironment—including macroeconomic policies; openness to trade; and stable, well-functioning political and legal institutions. The second is the microeconomic business environment—including the quality of the workforce and nonlabor inputs, infrastructure, institutions, and the array of regulatory and other policies that affect the way in which a nation's firms compete. The third factor is the operating practices and strategies of companies.

TCB activities aimed at enhancing economic responsiveness, competitiveness, and productivity are sometimes called "supply-side" or "behind-the-border" assistance. These activities may address a wide range of development needs in the public and private sectors—from helping governments create a competitive and enabling environment to supporting local enterprises' abilities to identify and produce goods and services the world is willing to buy.

Examples of projects in the public sector include

- increasing competition in transportation, telecommunications, and other trade-related service sectors.
- strengthening commercial law.
- developing the financial sector, including reforms in banking and securities markets and implementation of laws and regulations that protect and promote trade-related investment.

- strengthening competition policy and antitrust laws, and building institutional capacity to address anticompetitive monopolies.

Examples of projects in the private sector include:

- assisting sector and industry clusters to identify and address constraints to participation in international trade.
- developing efficient and competitive business development services, including enterprise and trade finance,[7] insurance, advertising, marketing, and freight forwarding services.
- improving agricultural producers' capacity to meet international sanitary and phytosanitary (SPS) standards and regulations.
- helping firms obtain and analyze international market information, linking them with international "enterprise networks" and developing local commercial and labor skills.
- remove barriers to the establishment and growth of small and medium-sized enterprises.

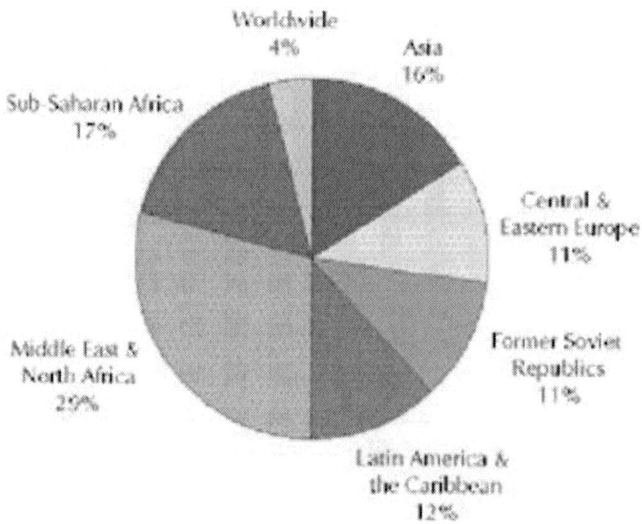

Figure 2. USAID TCB Funding by Region, 2001.

TCB projects often address two or all three of these strategic requirements. For example, a project that helps develop an efficient and competitive financial services sector may concurrently help prepare a country to participate in international negotiations on trade in services, implement existing agreements affecting that sector, build political consensus for participating in and implementing international agreements, and improve the competitiveness of other goods and services sectors that are dependent on high-quality, low-cost financial services.

Historically, the bulk of USAID TCB projects have focused on economic responsiveness, competitiveness, and productivity as the keys to raising living standards in developing countries. The Doha Development Agenda and other trade negotiations are increasing demand for assistance that addresses participation as well as implementation needs.

AN AGENCY-WIDE STRATEGY

USAID's TCB priorities need to be set at both agency and country levels. The selection and prioritization of TCB activities at the country level will continue to be determined by missions' country-specific strategic plans and resources. Priorities will vary from country to country, depending on levels of income and development, the quality of key leadership, geography, activities of other donors, the current and prospective composition of trade, and other important factors. In countries associated with specific trade negotiations or agreements, it will be important to consider needs identified in trade negotiations and through the interagency process.

At a global level, the agency's allocation of incremental TCB resources will be determined by its goal: to increase the number of developing and transition countries that are harnessing global economic forces to accelerate growth and increase incomes. TCB projects have the greatest promise for promoting rapid *integration* into the global economy when they are implemented in countries that already have made progress in establishing a commercial rule of law and liberalizing financial and other service sectors that support competitive exports. The projects are likely to have the greatest impact on *incomes* when they are implemented in reform-minded LDCs. In other low- and middle-income countries, TCB projects might have spillover benefits, helping generate economic growth in surrounding LDCs and other developing countries.

In this context, USAID will seek to direct new resources to TCB projects in countries where governments committed to reform and openness are in place or emerging. All else equal, USAID will give priority to reform-minded LDCs. The agency will also give precedence to other reform-minded, low-income countries (other than LDCs) when accelerated growth in those countries may have broad regional benefits for surrounding LDCs and other developing countries. In the context of ongoing trade negotiations, the agency will consider the need for assistance to improve the enabling environment for reform in countries that can play key roles in advancing U.S. trade liberalization initiatives. The prioritization of incremental resources under this strategy will not affect TCB projects that are implemented under other USAID strategic objectives, including projects in countries that do not fall in the categories described above.

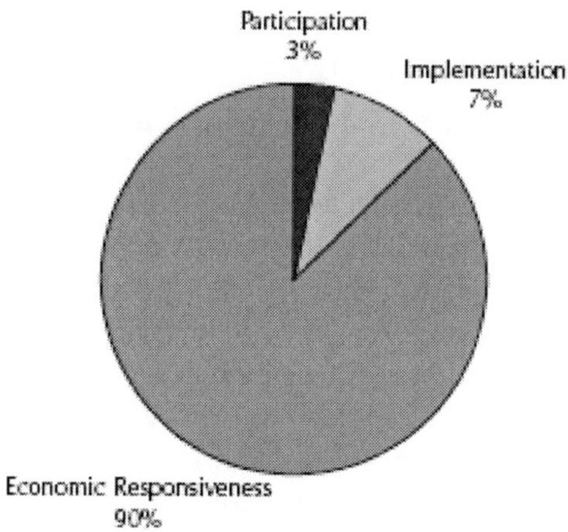

Figure 3. 2001 USAID TCB Funding by Category.

The agency will continue to support projects that address participation, implementation, and economic responsiveness. The bulk of overall TCB efforts will continue to focus on economic responsiveness to trade opportunities. At the same time, the agency must prepare itself to respond to increasing demand for projects that address challenges relating to developing countries' participation in trade negotiations and implementation of trade agreements. Many of these challenges may be identified in the course of trade negotiations. For this reason, it will be important for USAID and, in some cases, for individual missions to follow closely the substance and progress of global, regional, or bilateral trade negotiations and to coordinate with the U.S. Trade Representative (USTR) and the interagency process.

In support of developing countries' *participation* in international trade negotiations, USAID will

- increase support for developing and transition countries' efforts to accede to the WTO and participate in its consultations and negotiations.
- help countries develop the analytical expertise, information, and resources they need to participate more effectively in trade negotiations and global trade development.[8]
- strengthen USAID's in-house expertise and capabilities for responding to the growing demand for assistance related to participation in international negotiations.

To support the agency's field programs in this area, new USAID/Washington projects will

- distribute user-friendly trade data and analytical tools to a wide range of public and private sector users throughout the world.[9]
- strengthen the ability of African research institutions to conduct sophisticated analyses of national trade interests and provide policy-relevant recommendations to government decisionmakers.[10]

In support of efforts to *implement* international trade agreements, USAID will

- develop strategies and, as needed, create new mechanisms to support trade facilitation and customs reform, taking into account other donors' activities.
- support reform, liberalization, and increased efficiency in transportation, telecommunications, trade finance, marketing, and other services sectors that are critical to trade.

USAID/Washington will strengthen and catalyze field implementation projects by

- seeking to develop mechanisms to respond to unanticipated requests for short-term assistance needed to implement trade commitments/
- supporting efforts to comply with customs-related WTO requirements, including customs reform, reduction of customs clearance delays, and other trade facilitation measures, taking into account other donors' activities.[11]

- assisting in the privatization and creation of meaningful competition in key trade-related services sectors, in tandem with WTO negotiations on trade in services.[12]

USAID will continue to focus primarily on projects that strengthen and enhance developing countries' *economic responsiveness to trade opportunities.* To that end, the agency will

- continue to implement a broad range of trade-related economic growth projects, ranging from agricultural trade diversification and human resource development to commercial law and regulation, fiscal and financial sector reforms, and economic governance.
- assist developing countries seeking to take advantage of trade opportunities created by preferential market access programs such as those established by AGOA and the Andean Trade Promotion and Drug Eradication Act (ATPDEA).

USAID/Washington will help to strengthen field projects in this area through new programs that

- expand the use of USAID's successful commercial, legal, and institutional reform diagnostic tools, with particular focus on LDCs.
- support agricultural producers' capacity to meet food safety, pest management, and other SPS requirements in international markets.
- strengthen fiscal reforms that create growth-friendly tax regimes, reduce dependence on tariff revenues, and make room for continued tariff liberalization.
- foster the growth of business development services, trade finance, and other services industries that facilitate integration into the global economy.
- exploit the latest information technologies to create an "all-horizon" trade lead system to link developing country entrepreneurs with domestic and international business partners.

USAID must be opportunistic as well as strategic. In particular, the agency will look for opportunities where TCB projects can catalyze a range of mutually reinforcing political, economic, and social factors—including trade negotiations; international commercial networks; domestic political, legal, and governance reforms; and local economic capabilities and resources—to maximize their impact on economic growth and poverty. USAID will give top priority to projects that help generate local support for trade reforms, such as projects that mainstream trade into broader national development strategies.

USAID/Washington must be prepared to assist field missions in identifying and addressing these opportunities, particularly those emerging from international trade negotiations and initiatives. Therefore, USAID/Washington will facilitate the flow of policy and technical information to the missions. It will develop technical resources that assist missions to implement country-specific TCB projects in promising new fields, and support TCB assistance on a global or regional basis.

COUNTRY-LEVEL STRATEGIES

At the country level, a range of local trade and development issues needs to be cons ered—from the quality of staff at a ministry of trade to the strength of the business services that support producers, importers, and exporters. The Integrated Framework for Technical Assistance to LDCs (IF)13 is undertaking a series of diagnostic Integration and Competitiveness studies of LDCs.

Three such studies—in Madagascar, Cambodia, and Mauritania—have been completed, and 11 more are underway or planned through mid-2003. These studies (or studies modeled on them) can be a key resource for identifying local TCB needs. Also, with the ongoing FTA negotiations in the Western Hemisphere, USAID is assisting countries with their efforts to develop national TCB strategies as a vehicle for prioritizing their trade-related assistance needs and to mobilize donor, public, and private sector support. For example, within the FTAA, countries are preparing national TCB strategies to facilitate the mobilization of assistance resources under the Hemispheric Cooperation Program.

Though TCB needs will vary from country to country, in general the following apply:

- The poorer the country, the more comprehensive the range of TCB needs, though problems related to economic responsiveness, competitiveness, and productivity will likely be particularly acute.
- Customs procedures and customs clearance are problems in most developing countries.

- Transportation bottlenecks are often a significant impediment to developing countries' ability to respond to international demand; rural producers may be particularly affected.
- The capacity of LDC governments and small economies to manage trade participation and compliance requirements may be limited, so priorities must be set carefully.[14]
- In low-income countries, projects that support trade in agriculture are likely to have significant poverty reduction benefits.
- In LDCs and developing countries dependent on farm and fisheries products, producers lack awareness of and ability to meet foreign market requirements such as SPS standards.[15]

No universal prioritization or standard sequencing of TCB assistance applies to all countries. If analysis shows a country has largely implemented its WTO commitments, for example, attention may focus on economic responsiveness issues, and/or assisting the government to participate more effectively in trade policy development. If internal markets are too distorted for economic responsiveness approaches to generate reform from within support for participation in a regional trade agreement (RTA) or the WTO may elicit new pressures and new domestic sources of support for developmental change.

As in other areas of development assistance, the degree of political will and reform-minded leadership in support of particular TCB initiatives may ultimately prove the decisive factor in success. A variety of internal and external factors can be useful to galvanize local leadership. Interest groups such as exporters may generate pressure for change from within. The political imperative to join the EU or the WTO has motivated governments in Eastern Europe and Jordan to make major trade reforms. The IF can be a catalyst in LDCs. A political commitment to regional trade agreements—such as the Southern Africa Development Community—can provide momentum for trade-related improvements at home.

Thus, country-level TCB priorities should be assessed in the light of a wide range of trade and investment-related factors. However, the final choice of activities to support may need to be opportunistic as well. Where possible, USAID country missions should take advantage of and encourage the internal and external forces—such as membership in RTAs and the IF—that can catalyze local support for trade-related change.

Specific Considerations

A number of specific considerations will influence the agency's approach to TCB.

- Least developed countries: Concentrated in Africa, LDCs are the most marginalized from the global economic system. They account for one-fifth of the membership of the WTO, and the United States has a stake in addressing their concerns. USAID will give priority to LDCs with strong reform leadership.
- Integrated Framework: The IF provides a focal point for reinforcing LDC reforms and coordinating TCB activities among donors. USAID country missions will be encouraged to incorporate the outcome of IF diagnostics in formulating their country strategies and to support follow-on projects identified as priorities in IF diagnostic reports. USAID may continue to make modest contributions to the IF Trust Fund to support additional diagnostic studies, but the agency's principal support to the IF will be in the form of follow-on TCB projects under the agency's bilateral programs.
- Large-scale physical infrastructure projects: Roads, ports, airports, rail transport, telecommunications, and other physical infrastructure are essential for improved trade and investment. Direct USAID finance for large-scale infrastructure will be limited. But where such lack of infrastructure is a critical constraint, the agency will seek opportunities to facilitate the development of ownership and management structures and to strengthen the legal and competitive environment to attract other funds, particularly from the private sector. In some cases, USAID will serve in a technical advisory role for large infrastructure projects being planned by other donors.
- *Trade and labor:* The development record indicates that rapid growth in trade—particularly in exports—is typically associated with increased demand for labor (especially unskilled labor), higher wages, and more and better employment opportunities. Part of USAID's work in the area of competitiveness and productivity promotes well-functioning labor markets, including a flexible, qualified, and mobile workforce. Labor issues raised in the context of trade (but extending well beyond trade to other production activity) include core labor standards, child labor, trafficking of persons, and safety nets for

displaced workers. Programs in a number of U.S. Government agencies—particularly the Department of Labor and USAID—address these issues. As required in legislation granting the president trade promotion authority and echoed in the recently issued National Security Strategy, the United States will incorporate labor concerns into U.S. trade negotiations and will use the International Labor Organization, trade preference programs, and trade talks to improve working conditions in conjunction with freer trade.

- *Trade and gender:* Along with the concerns mentioned above, gender considerations are part of a more general concern about links between trade and poverty. More specifically, the concern is that the poor—especially poor women—are in a weak position to take advantage of the economic opportunities provided by trade because of inadequate education and training and limited access to assets such as credit. On the general issue of trade and poverty, a recent review of research indicates that the economic growth generated by expanded openness and trade tends to benefit all income groups proportionately to their incomes, with no discernible impact on income distribution. Thus, the general expectation based on the empirical record is that if overall income rises by 10 percent, income of the poor will also rise by 10 percent, despite the disadvantages that the poor face.[16]

  A separate review of research more specifically focused on gender concludes that "the direct effect of trade expansion on employment opportunities and wages appears generally to favor women, particularly in manufacturing and service sectors. Although the jobs pay significantly less than they pay in the developed countries,they usually pay more than the local 'going rate.'"[17] The research stresses the importance of investments in human capital in the form of education and training so that women can better take advantage of the opportunities generated by increased trade. USAID emphasizes such programs, as well as programs that increase access of women to credit and other assets in its overall approach to development.
- *Trade and environment:* Trade-led economic growth and poverty reduction strategies must be pursued in the broader context of sustainable development. Trade capacity building and efforts to improve environmental protection and sustainable resource management are mutually reinforcing. Projects that raise incomes in communities located in highly stressed rural agricultural ecosystems and that promote the development of ecotourism are important

examples. USAID TCB activities will seek to take advantage of such win-win opportunities. As required in the Trade Act of 2002, which granted the president trade promotion authority, and as was echoed in the *National Security Strategy,* the United States will incorporate environmental concerns into U.S. trade negotiations.

- *Availability of discretionary economic growth funds:* Funding for most USAID trade and investment capacity building programs comes from the agency's Economic Growth (EG) budget. Except for the Europe and Eurasia region and Economic Support Fund-supported country missions, access to discretionary EG funds is limited, particularly for the reform-minded LDCs prioritized in this strategy. USAID will explore the potential for increasing the EG budget to expand capacity building activities and reach priority countries.
- *Support for the Doha Development Agenda and other trade initiatives:* The timetables for the Doha Development Agenda, the FTAA, and other trade negotiations imply a rapid increase in TCB activities within a shorter period than normal planning and implementation cycles. The administration expects USAID to be responsive and to react in the context of the negotiating timetable. Developing countries and parts of the administration also expect TCB assistance to produce tangible results in a short timeframe. USAID will need to accelerate delivery of TCB assistance and seek additional TCB-related funding in FY2003 and FY2004, when multilateral and regional trade negotiations will be intense. Given the normal pace of institutional change and structural adjustment in LDCs, it may be difficult to demonstrate dramatic and tangible outcomes in the short timeframe of ongoing trade negotiations. The agency will therefore need to set ambitious but realistic objectives for its IF followup projects.
- *Regional trade arrangements:* USAID will actively assist developing countries pursuing bilateral or regional trade arrangements with the United States. Participation in multilateral trade initiatives and other trade agreements involving both developed and developing countries is likely to contribute more to economic growth than will RTAs between developing countries alone. In some cases, regional cooperation between developing countries on technical issues (e.g., standards testing and certification), customs unions, and other RTAs may reinforce multilateral liberalization, promote investment, and bolster reforms. Experience suggests, however, that USAID should

proceed cautiously with projects that are exclusively focused on regional activities in which there is no developed country participation. In particular, it is important to ensure that RTAs will not distort trade, and that the political commitment of participating governments is sufficient to ensure effective and sustained implementation.

- *Preferential trade agreements:* Many developed countries provide preferential access to LDC products through such programs as the U.S. Generalized System of Preferences (GSP), the ATPDEA, the Caribbean Basin Initiative, and AGOA. The EU, Australia, Canada, Japan, and New Zealand also have GSP-type programs. In addition, the EU has the Cotonou Partnership Agreement and Everything But Arms (EBA) initiatives. But these arrangements are complex, and developing countries (governments and private sector entities) often lack the capacity to comply with requirements such as licensing or rules of origin. USAID will assist developing countries to take particular advantage of U.S. preferential access programs such as AGOA, but it will also assist them to take advantage of opportunities to gain access to other markets.
- *Coordination with other U.S. agencies:* Because of the growing overlap between trade and development, USAID and the trade policy agencies need to work together closely to coordinate U.S. responses to developing country requests for TCB assistance. As part of this process, some missions will need to be involved in interagency discussions and decisions on TCB needs relating to specific ongoing trade negotiations. An agreed USAID TCB strategy should help focus and inform the agency's participation in interagency meetings. Nonetheless, increased coordination with other agencies, the increasing number of trade negotiations, and acceleration of negotiation schedules will place large new demands on staff.[18] In addition to USAID, 14 U.S. Government agencies provide TCB assistance to developing countries. USAID should take a primary role in coordinating assistance among these agencies.
- *Contribution to trade policy:* USAID does not make trade policy but focuses on TCB assistance. Because many trade policies have a significant impact on development, USAID will, as it deems necessary, contribute its development perspective within the U.S. interagency framework for trade policy.

- *Coordination with other donors:* Multilateral development banks, development institutions, trade institutions, and bilateral donors are increasingly providing TCB assistance. Coordination among donors—both in capitals and in the field—is essential to avoid redundancy and to leverage funds. But donor coordination is also staff intensive, and additional staff resources will be required to support the level of coordination required. To the extent that coordinating institutions such as the IF exist, USAID will support them.

NEXT STEPS

The decentralized nature of USAID programming means that most USAID TCB projects will be conceived and managed in the field. Success will require strengthening the trade knowledge and expertise of field staff, sharpening the trade focus of field programs, and providing technical leadership in the area of best practices and global innovation. Accordingly, in addition to the initiatives discussed above, USAID will mainstream trade into the agency's planning and programs at all levels by the following:

- *Enhancing trade knowledge and skills.* Trade training sessions and workshops for staff have already started, covering trade theory and trends, trade institutions, and TCB. Over 80 staff have completed an intensive two-day course, and another 80 will complete the course by the end of 2002. The course will be offered to an additional 80 staff per year through 2004. More than 20 senior staff have completed a half-day workshop on trade and development, and additional workshops are planned.
- *Requiring country strategies to consider trade and investment.* In consultation with USAID country missions and the regional bureaus, the Bureaus for Policy and Program Coordination and Economic Growth, Agriculture and Trade (EGAT) will develop appropriate guidelines for this process and will offer the analytical tools to help missions examine the role of trade in their countries and make strategic choices.
- *Developing best-practice trade and investment tools.* EGAT will develop technical resources and tools that can be adapted to country

or regional needs and deployed quickly and cost effectively in the field.

- *Communicating capacity building needs identified by USAID/Washington.* Given the centralized nature of trade negotiations, it is likely that some capacity building needs will be identified at the negotiating table and communicated to USAID/Washington. Headquarters will provide information on such needs to the field for appropriate integration into missions' ongoing TCB strategies and projects.

Regional Initiatives

USAID TCB activities have been widely and fairly evenly distributed throughout the developing world. A variety of new region-specific TCB initiatives are under way or planned. These are particularly important and high profile in Africa and Latin America, where they complement and support AGOA, FTAA, and an anticipated free trade agreement with Central America. Region-specific initiatives and anticipated regional patterns in USAID's TCB programs are summarized in Appendix 3.

Assessing Progress

USAID's progress in implementing this strategy will be measured on several levels.

- In the short term, more developing countries will accede to the WTO; those that are or become WTO members will effectively implement an increased number of WTO obligations. Developing countries will put into place specific trade- and investment-inducing reforms.
- Missions will have an increasing number of active trade-related programs that will reflect USAID staff's increased knowledge and sophistication in trade issues. The programs will respond to the needs of host countries and to the timetables of ongoing trade negotiations.
- Developing countries will become more active, better informed participants in the Doha Development Agenda negotiations. They will recognize that they are getting increased levels of assistance and that

such assistance is enabling them to participate more effectively in multilateral negotiations.

- TCB activities will produce tangible results in individual countries. For example, government-owned utilities or transport facilities will be privatized; customs clearance times will be shortened; and commercial, legal, and institutional frameworks will be strengthened.
- Over time, the quantity and—more importantly—the quality of developing countries' exports, imports, and foreign investments will improve. The quality of trade can be measured by increasing diversification of a developing country's production and consumption of traded goods and services, both for products and for markets and sources. It may also be measured by the value added to exports. The principal indicator of the quality of investment will simply be a measure of FDI flows.

Funding

The success of U.S. trade negotiations and the developmental impact of TCB rely on a significant increase in USAID TCB assistance during the next few years, in tandem with Doha, FTAA, and other negotiations. Funding for an expanded program in FY2003 and FY2004, including the activities described above, is essential and must be identified and secured.

Working with Other U.S. Government Agencies

USAID funds 75 percent of total U.S. TCB assistance overseas. This reflects the agency's conviction that trade is a critical factor for development. Fourteen other federal agencies also contribute.[19] Many of these are funded by USAID through 632(a) and 632(b) Interagency Agreements.

USAID will continue to rely on expertise provided by private sector contractors and nongovernmental organizations in implementing most of its TCB projects. However, in areas such as competition policy, customs reform, food safety regulation, and intellectual property rights protection, U.S. Government personnel may be the most appropriate providers of TCB assistance. In response to such needs, USAID/Washington will work with country missions to harness the unique capabilities of other government agencies in support of this strategy.

To maintain close and regular communications on TCB issues between trade and development agencies and between USAID/Washington and the missions, EGAT will continue to co-chair an interagency working group on trade-related technical assistance and will disseminate information on U.S. trade policy, trade negotiations, and the current activities of other U.S. Government agencies in trade capacity building to other USAID bureaus and missions.

APPENDIX 1

Project Categories Identified in the FY2002 U.S. Survey of TCB Activities

Beginning in the summer of 2001, the U.S. Government conducted two surveys of its programs and activities that promote trade capacity building in developing and transition economies around the world. Activities included in the most recent survey, reflecting TCB projects funded under the FY 2002 federal budget, were reported in the categories shown below. These categories are comprehensive and include TCB implemented by USAID and 15 other federal agencies. Because they were developed to establish a baseline of data on government-wide activities, the categories do not necessarily correspond to the conceptual framework set out in this strategy.

Trade facilitation is generally defined as assistance in lowering the costs of engaging in or eliminating obstacles to international trade flows. In the USAID survey of U.S. Government initiatives in trade capacity building, trade facilitation is reported as the sum of the following six subcategories:

- *Customs operation and administration* is assistance to help countries modernize and improve the performance of their customs services.
- *E-Commerce development and information technologies (IT)* includes assistance to help countries acquire and use IT to promote trade by creating business networks and disseminating market information.
- *Exp ort promotion* includes assistance to increase market opportunities for developing country and transition economy producers.

- *Business services and training* includes support to improve the associations and networks in the business sector as well as to enhance the skills of business people engaged in trade.
- *Regional trade agreement (RTA) capacity building* includes assistance to an RTA or to an individ ual country that increases the ability of the RTA to facilitate trade. It can also include assistance to a potential member of an RTA that improves the analytical capacity of the country's government with respect to RTA issues.[20]
- *Other trade facilitation* includes support to increase trade flows that is not categorized in one of the other five subcategories.

Human resources and labor standards assistance helps support the enforcement of labor standards and worker rights, development of trade unions and dispute resolution mechanisms, strategies for workforce development and worker training, and the elimination of child labor.

Physical infrastructure development assistance helps establish trade-related telecommunication, transport, ports, airports, power, water, and industrial zones.

Trade-related agricultural development assistance supports trade-related aspects of the agriculture and agribusiness sector.[21]

Environmental sector trade and standards assistance establishes environmental standards or promote environmental technology.

Governance/transparency and interagency coordination includes support for institutional reform to improve governance and make policies more transparent, as well as assistance to help the different agencies of a host country government function more effectively in the trade policy arena.

Financial sector development and good governance assistance includes financial sector work, monetary and fiscal policy, exchange rates, commodity markets, and capital markets.

Competition policy and foreign investment assistance supports the design and implementation of antitrust laws, and laws and regulations related to investment and investor protections.

Services trade development includes support to help developing and transition economies increase their flows of trade in services. Services trade development is the sum of the assistance in the following two subcategories:

- *Tourism sector development* includes assistance to help countries expand their international tourism sectors, including ecotourism.

- *Other services development* includes assistance to help countries develop trade in services in all sectors other than tourism, including financial services, energy, transportation, and education.

WTO awareness and accession assistance is the sum of support in the following two subcategories:

- *WTO awareness and participation* assistance helps governments and private sector institutions benefit from membership in the WTO or understand fully the benefits of membership.
- *WTO accession* includes assistance to help countries in the WTO accession process to meet the requirements of accession.

Specific WTO agreements includes assistance that enables countries to better implement and benefit from particular WTO agreements. The U.S. survey reports TCB projects related to the WTO Agreement on Customs Valuation, Agreement on Agriculture, Agreement on the Application of Sanitary and Phytosanitary Measures, Agreement on Trade-Related Aspects of Intellectual Property Rights, General Agreement on Trade in Services, and 12 other WTO agreements. Assistance relating to these agreements often helps developing countries build the capacity to participate in negotiations and implement similar agreements made in other regional and bilateral forums.

APPENDIX 2

Conditions Conducive to Trade and Investment in Developing Countries

Political and Security Environment

- A stable and secure nation free from territorial, ethnic, religious, social, or other sources of internal or external instability
- Leadership committed to market-oriented reform

Macroeconomic Environment

- A stable and transparent currency regime and a competitive exchange rate

- A diversified base of production (industrial, agricultural, raw materials) that is not excessively dependent on a limited number of products or markets
- Low inflation
- Availability of private and public savings (domestic or foreign) to fund needed investment, particularly in physical infrastructure and human capacity development

Trade Environment

- Effective trade institutions, including an interministerial coordinating mechanism:
  - qualified, trained staff sufficient to handle the trade-related needs of their institutions
  - institutional mechanism for ensuring effective public-private sector collaboration, exchange of ideas, and evaluation of policy options
  - no state monopoly over trade in goods and services
  - availability of accurate trade data (for imports and exports) to permit trade-remedy actions to stave off import surges, or to slow or cease exports to avoid trade-remedy actions against exporters
- Membership in the WTO and regional trade arrangements, as appropriate:
  - compliance with obligations
  - effective participation in negotiations
  - regional/provincial compliance with and enforcement of trade laws
- Bilateral trade agreements or preferential trade agreements with trading partners:
  - private-sector awareness and ability to meet requirements of preferential trading arrangements (e.g., GSP, AGOA, EBA)
- Availability of low-cost production inputs: - low import tariffs, simplified tariff structure
  - no nontariff barriers, including registration requirements, for imports and exports
  - access to duty-free production inputs (e.g. through duty drawback, bonded warehouse, free trade zone, or other schemes)
- Low transactions costs:
  - liberalization of key services sectors (GATS obligations and country schedules)

  - efficient, predictable, and transparent customs processing for needed inputs and exports (in compliance with Harmonized Tariff System, Customs Valuation Agreement, WTO Agreement on Rules of Origin, and other international customs rules)
  - expeditious import and export clearance procedures
  - risk-management procedures for any preshipment inspection requirements
  - availability of trade facilitation services (warehousing, marketing, market research)
- National technical standards that conform to international practices and procedures:
  - private sector awareness of and ability to comply with, standards affecting key exports to key markets
- Availability of trade financing and export credits
- Transparent, open, competitive public procurement processes
- Trade promotion organizations, chambers of commerce, industry associations

Investment Environment

- Transparency and predictability of investment regime, consistent with international rules and conventions:
  - membership in and compliance with multilateral and regional trade and investment agreements
  - national treatment for domestic and foreign investors
  - effective protection of intellectual property rights
  - protection of persons and property from expropriation
  - repatriation of profits permitted and guaranteed
  - transfer of assets permitted and guaranteed
  - formalized dispute resolution process
  - bilateral investment treaties
  - accession to international conventions on arbitration and the enforcement of arbitral awards
- Streamlined, efficient administrative processes:
  - expeditious investment approval, licensing, permits
  - one-stop shop for foreign investors (government-sponsored foreign investment advisory body)
- Investment incentives (e.g., taxes, import duties, loans, hiring and firing of labor, access to land and utilities): - export promotion zones

- Availability of low-cost inputs (including imports):
  - efficiency, predictability of customs processing of imported inputs/exports
- Receptivity to foreign investment (limited, clearly identified exclusions):
  - privatization of public entities in a transparent, competitive, and equitable manner in which foreign participation is permitted
  - receptivity to a variety of forms of foreign investment, including majority foreign ownership and wholly owned foreign enterprises

Commercial and Regulatory Environment

- Commercial banking regime that provides funds to finance investment (including long-term investment); lends on the basis of creditworthiness of the borrowers, with risk-adjusted interest rates that represent the opportunity cost of capital, combined with a collateral system that facilitates commercial lending by creating recognized security interests in assets; includes adequate prudential and supervisory institutions and policies
- Company law regime allowing for market entry and operation and that defines norms for the organization of formal commercial activities by two or more individuals
- Competition policy regime that preserves competition in the market place by regulating or proscribing cartels and other anticompetitive behavior
- Contract law regime that creates, interprets, and enforces commercial obligations between parties
- Bankruptcy law regime that facilitates the orderly liquidation of outstanding financial claims by creditors against companies
- Other commercial laws and regulations influencing the production and sale of goods and services, such as
  - the hiring and firing of labor and worker rights
  - land ownership and other property rights - price controls
  - good governance (antibribery and anticorruption)
  - environmental protection/sustainable development policies
  - internationally accepted accounting standards
- Tax laws and regulations ensuring the fair, transparent, and equitable collection of taxes by national and local government entities

Market Participants (Institutions and Human Resources)

- A pool of skilled and trained labor and management
- Social safety net, retraining, and transition assistance to encourage reintegration into the workforce of dislocated workers
- Market-responsive producers (agriculture, industry, raw materials, and services) eager to develop export capacity and responsive to market conditions (including standards, competition, fashion, and quality); market-responsive (upstream) suppliers of inputs; (downstream) marketers, distributors, and exporters of production
- Producer organizations (agriculture, industry, raw materials, and services) that can exchange information on foreign market conditions and provide input to government officials charged with formulating and implementing commercial and trade policy
- Business development services that can provide support to private enterprise (e.g., accounting firms, lawyers, marketing firms, advertising firms, and business consultants)

Infrastructure

- Availability of efficient, low-cost, internal, and crossborder transportation links, including roads, rail, airports, and port facilities to permit efficient transport of export goods and necessary production inputs
- Availability of related distribution services, including cold storage facilities, warehouses, and express delivery services
- Availability of telecommunications links (both internal and crossborder)
- Availability of reliable, competitively priced power supplies and distribution networks

Access to Foreign Markets

- Access to foreign markets for goods and services the developing country produces

Appendix 3. Regional Trade Capacity Building Initiatives

Asia and Near East

TCB is a growing priority in the Asia and Near East (ANE) bureau. USAID is supporting an increasing number of bilateral agreements, continuing ongoing support for WTO implementation and preparation for the Cancun Ministerial, and supporting the development agenda through behindthe-border and beyond-the-border activities.

Bilateral agreements with countries such as Morocco, Jordan, and Vietnam have recently taken the stage. The United States and Morocco began negotiating FTA in 2002. USAID will support this process by helping identify TCB needs related to the negotiation, implement an FTA, and enhance Moroccan producers' ability to take advantage of the trade and investment opportunities created by an FTA. USAID has also assisted with the negotiation and implementation of the Jordan Free Trade Agreement and the Vietnam Bilateral Trade Agreement, which were signed in 2000 and 2001, respectively.

USAID support for WTO accession and implementation reflects a steady, ongoing commitment. In preparation for the Cancun Ministerial, USAID assistance is helping countries better understand and prepare for trade negotiations and better meet WTO commitments, especially customs valuation, SP measures, trade-related aspects of intellectual property rights (TRIPS), and technical barriers to trade. USAID supports this kind of long-term work in countries such as the Philippines, Indonesia, and Jordan. In the Philippines, USAID TCB activities highlight the link between good governance and trade standards. In Lebanon, USAID is helping the government raise public awareness on and accede to the WTO by the end of 2003. Vietnam also has a goal of acceding to the WTO by 2005. In Cambodia, USAID supports the IF (an item of the Doha development agenda) by assisting civil societies to advocate trade reform.

USAID aims to better integrate TCB into developing countries' development agendas and poverty reduction strategies. While market access depends on at-the-border and beyond-the-border work involving trade agreements, such work does not bring about effective participation in global markets or meet concerns expressed by developing countries at Doha. USAID promotes a broad range of behind-the-border activities to help improve the capacity of countries to trade in the ANE region and in the rest of the world.

These include programs that support competitiveness in Sri Lanka and Mongolia, financial market reform in India and Southeast Asia, and information and communication technology in Jordan, Egypt, Bangladesh, and the Philippines.

Europe and Eurasia

Throughout Europe and Eurasia, USAID continues to focus trade- and investment-related assistance on facilitating the sustainable integration of countries into the global economy. In broad terms, USAID will continue efforts to help transition countries establish market economies by creating an enabling environment for trade and investment, develop commercial laws and implementing institutions, promote competitive industries and clusters, and reform banking systems and financial markets. These measures are expected, among other things, to promote foreign direct investment inflows and increase intraregional trade.

The Europe and Eurasia (E&E) bureau manages the TRADE (Trading Regionally and Developing Expertise) Network in southeastern Europe, which seeks to develop crossborder trade and investment and regional business integration by facilitating trade linkages. This is accomplished through a network of consultants and business support institutions in Bulgaria, Croatia, Romania, and Hungary. The European TRADE Network seeks to strengthen the capacity of businesses in the region to meet international standards (including ISO compliance) and attract international investment. In addition, the network addresses common constraints to growth of regional businesses and develops partnerships to take advantage of crossborder business opportunities.

The E&E bureau has also launched an agro-industry competitiveness initiative to facilitate increased competitiveness of agricultural industries and clusters in the region. The program will assist entrepreneurs to judge the competitiveness of their products in domestic, regional, and international markets. It will also identify areas of cooperation within the sector to improve overall competitiveness as countries anticipate WTO membership and EU accession. The program will also provide a forum to discuss common constraints to trade and growth for agricultural markets. Finally, competitiveness assessments are being completed in a number of E&E countries to identify competitive sectors, sub-sectors, and industries, and to identify potential competitiveness activities for USAID missions.

At the country level, several USAID programs address the issue of competitiveness. This is accomplished through support to clusters and facilitating efforts at the national level to improve overall competitiveness. USAID/Macedonia recently launched a major initiative to focus national efforts on improving the country's overall competitiveness and enhancing its enterprises through support to industry clusters. Similar activities at the national level are underway in Bulgaria, Croatia, and Kosovo; others are contemplated for Russia and Central Asia. Other activities focus on support for firm-level performance and productivity improvement, as well as the facilitation of trade and investment linkages through regional trade fairs and other business-to-business opportunities. Finally, USAID maintains numerous small- and mid-sized enterprise (SME) credit and technical assistance programs throughout the region. One activity in Kazakhstan is working to enhance quality management services—including ISO compliance—for SMEs that serve the energy sector.

A number of capacity building programs focus on providing technical assistance to facilitate accession to the WTO. Twelve countries in the region are seeking accession: Armenia, Azerbaijan, Belarus, Bosnia Herzegovina, Kazakhstan, the Former Yugoslav Republic of Macedonia, Russia, Tajikistan, Ukraine, Uzbekistan, and the Federal Republic of Yugoslavia. Many of these countries will receive USAID technical assistance with WTO awareness and accession.

For the countries of Central and Eastern Europe, the process has also involved entry into the EU. Ten countries in the region are in line to join. Two—Bulgaria and Romania—receive significant USAID assistance that focuses on key gaps with respect to EU membership, including judicial reform and SME development. The remaining eight countries—Poland, the Czech Republic, Slovakia, Slovenia, Hungary, Estonia, Latvia, and Lithuania—all graduates of USAID assistance, continue to receive USAID support to facilitate EU membership, particularly in financial sector reform. Through the Partnership for Financial Stability, USAID is assisting these countries to reform their respective financial sectors in order to meet EU entry requirements.

At the country level, USAID is providing significant levels of assistance to reform national financial sectors. Banking reform and/or capital market development projects are underway in Armenia, Georgia, Kazakhstan, Kyrgyzstan, Uzbekistan, Ukraine, Bulgaria, Romania, Croatia, and Bosnia. The focus of these activities is on bank supervision, bank accounting, and transparent capital market operations.

Fiscal reform is another major area of USAID assistance throughout Europe and Eurasia. Typically, USAID activities support improved fiscal policy environments in recipient countries, and focus on tax policy, tax administration, performance-based budgeting, and intergovernmental finance. Fiscal reform activities are underway in Croatia, Kosovo, Serbia, Montenegro, Russia, Kazakhstan, Kyrgyzstan, Uzbekistan, Armenia, and Georgia.

A major challenge continues to be integration into the global economy of the economies of Eurasia (the former Soviet Union, excluding the Baltics). Many countries remain relatively autarchic, or strongly linked to Russia, or both, with relatively few economic ties to the rest of the world. Further, because the export sectors in some of these countries (Russia and Kazakhstan, for example) are heavily dependent on natural resources such as energy, minerals, and agriculture, the countries are vulnerable (or potentially so) to volatile fluctuations in commodity prices. In Central Asia, USAID has initiated a series of trade facilitation programs to assist Kazakhstan, Uzbekistan, and Tajikistan to accede to the WTO. Meanwhile, USAID continues to assist Kyrgyzstan fulfill its post-entry WTO requirements. Activities include a customs modernization project, development of common standards to facilitate crossborder trade, removal of investment constraints, and launch of a new regional trade network.

Latin America and Caribbean

The Latin America and Caribbean (LAC) bureau is expanding its subregional and bilateral trade and investment capacity building programs, in response to 1) approaching negotiation deadlines for the FTAA and the Doha Round and the launching of negotiations for CAFTA; and 2) mounting requirements for assistance in implementing agreements resulting from these negotiations. All LAC countries except the Bahamas are already members of the WTO. USAID support for TCB in the region is focused on assisting countries to prepare for trade negotiations, implement trade agreements, and enhance competitiveness in world trade.

In the Caribbean, USAID is building on Secretary of State Colin Powell's Third Border Initiative to strengthen partner countries' trade and investment capacities, including support for consensus- building activities involving the public and private sectors. The program is being led by USAID/Jamaica's Caribbean Regional Program.

In Central America, USAID is working through the rural development Opportunity Alliance initiative to support partner country efforts to prepare for and participate in the negotiation of CAFTA. The program is being led by USAID/ Guatemala's Office for Central American Programs. USAID is also working with other donors to develop assistance programs to respond to national TCB priorities as identified in the national strategies of the Central American countries. These strategies were developed to help the countries prepare for the U.S.-CAFTA negotiations. In addition, USAID will continue to work with other LAC countries developing country strategies under the FTAA Hemispheric Cooperation Program.

In South America, USAID is implementing the Andean Regional TCB Program to assist the five Andean Community countries to meet WTO obligations (e.g., SPS), enhance competition policy investigation and enforcement, and address other priority TCB needs identified by USAID in consultation with the Andean countries. The program is being led by USAID/Peru.

Individual bilateral missions also are ramping up their support for TCB, while USAID/Washington has put in place a new "quick response" mechanism to give it the flexibility to respond rapidly to TCB needs where the required response cannot be met in a timely manner through existing subregional, bilateral, or central programs and mechanisms.

Sub-Saharan Africa

Comprising predominantly LDCs, sub-Saharan Africa (SSA) will continue to require significant USAID assistance in trade and investment capacity building. Most SSA countries are already members of the WTO. Only Cape Verde, Sudan, and Seychelles are seeking to accede, although Ethiopia, Eritrea, Equatorial Guinea, and São Tomé (all currently WTO observers) may seek to join the WTO as well. WTO-related assistance will therefore focus primarily on enabling countries to participate more effectively in the ongoing negotiations, identify their national interest with respect to policy options, and achieve domestic consensus. Many SSA WTO members also need assistance in complying with their trade commitments. Other TCB assistance will focus on behind-the-border activities.

The IF diagnostics will be particularly important in identifying priorities in individual countries, as many of these countries are undergoing an IF diagnostic study. USAID activities will blend country-specific programs with support for regional trade groupings. USAID assistance will also complement AGOA, which provides qualifying countries preferential access to the U.S. market.

President Bush's new Trade for African Development and Enterprise initiative (TRADE) will promote U.S.-African business linkages, enhance the competitiveness of African products and services, expand the role that trade plays in African poverty reduction strategies, improve the delivery of public services supporting trade, build African capacity for trade policy formulation and implementation, and strengthen the enabling environment for African businesses. One of its first activities is to fund Regional Hubs for Global Competitiveness, located at USAID's three regional missions in Ghana, Kenya, and Botswana. Beginning in 2003, TRADE (Africa) funding will be available for programs in individual countries. It is anticipated that IF diagnostic studies and the new worldwide trade activities already described will be useful in identifying activities for TRADE funding.

Abbreviations and Acronyms

AGOA	African Growth and Opportunity Act
ANE	Asia and Near East (USAID bureau)
APEC	Asia Pacific Economic Cooperation
ATPDEA	Andean Trade Promotion and Drug Eradication Act
CAFTA	Central American Free Trade Area
EBA	Everything But Arms
E&E	Europe and Eurasia (USAID bureau)
EG	economic growth (USAID budget)
EGAT	Economic Growth, Agriculture and Trade (USAID bureau)
FDI	foreign direct investment
FTA	Free Trade Agreement
FTAA	Free Trade Area of the Americas
GSP	U.S. Generalized System of Preferences
IF	Integrated Framework for Technical Assistance
LAC	Latin American and Caribbean (USAID bureau)
LDC	least developed country
RTA	regional trade agreement
SME	small- and mid-sized enterprise
SPS	sanitary and phytosanitary
TCB	trade capacity building
TRADE (Africa)	Trade for African Development and Enterprise

TRADE (Europe)Trading Regionally and Developing Expertise
USTR U.S. Trade Representative

End Notes

[1] World Bank, Globalization, Growth, and Poverty: Building an Inclusive World Economy (Washington, DC: World Bank, 2002).

[2] See <www.whitehouse.gov/nsc/nss.html>.

[3] World Trade Organization, International Trade Statistics, 2001 (Geneva: WTO, 2001).

[4] For example, in 2000, China, Hong Kong, and Brazil accounted for over 50 percent of total FDI to developing economies, and the top 10 developing economy recipients of FDI absorbed 77 percent of the total flows. The 49 LDCs absorbed just 0.3 percent of the global FDI inflows and just 1.6 percent of the total FDI inflows to developing countries in 2000. United Nations Conference on Trade and Development, World Investment Report 2001 (Geneva: UNCTAD, September 2001).

[5] See <www.dec.org/pdf_docs/PNACN110.pdf.>

[6] See USAID Policy Determinations 20 and 71, <www.usaid.gov/pubs/ads/300/pd20.pdf> and <www.usaid.gov/pubs/ads/200/pd71.pdf>.

[7] Where financial systems are particularly weak, USAID's Development Credit Authority may be able to play a catalytic role in expanding access to trade finance.

[8] For example, USAID's regional program in Central America is helping five countries build needed analytical expertise and skills for negotiations on a U.S.-Central American Free Trade Area (CAFTA) Agreement and negotiations on the FTAA.

[9] These analytical resources include trade flow and trade barrier information that can be used to identify and analyze market opportunities.

[10] This has been one of the most frequently raised needs by developing country WTO members at Doha and subsequent WTO consultations.

[11] Trade diagnostic studies consistently identify customs problems as being among the top two or three most serious TCB constraints.

[12] Support for the privatization of Kenya National Railways is an early example.

[13] The IF was established by WTO trade ministers in 1997 to promote the integration of LDCs into the global economy. Participating agencies include the WTO, the International Monetary Fund, the International Trade Centre, the United Nations Development Program, the United Nations Conference on Trade and Development, and the World Bank.

[14] In many LDCs, there are only a few key individuals who must handle all trade-related negotiations—multilaterally, regionally, and bilaterally. Many LDCs do not have a trade mission in Geneva to assist with WTO-related negotiations. Further, the ability of LDCs and small economies to manage simultaneously complex negotiations and implementation tasks is impeded by high turnover among staff and illness (particularly in countries with a high incidence of HIV/AIDs).

[15] Quality control issues, including those related to SPS standards in target export markets, were noted as significant impediments to export competitiveness in the IF diagnostic studies of Madagascar, Mauritania, and Cambodia.

[16] Andrew Berg and Anne Krueger, "Trade, Growth, and Poverty," prepared for the Annual World Bank Conference on Development Economics, April 2002, <www.econ.world bank.org/files/13377_Berg_and_ Krueger. pdf>

[17] Samuel Skogstad, "International Trade: Impact, Opportunities and Constraints on the Participation of Women—A Review of Empirical Research," prepared for USAID's Office of Women in Development.

[18] TCB needs are being discussed in a growing number of trade negotiating forums, including the WTO, the FTAA, APEC, trade agreements under the Stability Pact in the Balkans, and bilateral negotiations envisaged under U.S. trade initiatives like the CAFTA, the U.S.-Morocco Free Trade Area, and the Southern Africa Free Trade and Development Agreement. The U.S. Trade Representative has 60 interagency subcommittees of the Trade Policy Staff Committee, many of which require USAID participation. Ad hoc participation or briefings of the 33 USTR private sector advisory committees are also likely.

[19] The 14 federal agencies are: Department of Energy, Department of Justice, Federal Trade Commission, Food and Drug Administration, Environmental Protection Agency, Department of the Interior, Small Business Administration, the U.S. Peace Corps, Department of Commerce (National Institute for Standards and Technology, Patent and Trademark Office), Department of the Treasury, Trade and Development Agency, Department of Agriculture, Department of Labor, and Department of State.

[20] It does not include TCB assistance in a specific area that is being provided to countries through an RTA. For example, technical assistance to help RTA member countries comply with SPS standards should be reported as trade-related agricultural development or the WTO Agreement on SPS Standards.

[21] Support intended to help countries participate in the WTO Agreement on Agriculture or SPS standards is reported separately.

INDEX

C

D

E

F

G

H

I

N

O

P

Q

R

U

V

W

Y

Z